Business Guides on the Go

"Business Guides on the Go" presents cutting-edge insights from practice on particular topics within the fields of business, management, and finance. Written by practitioners and experts in a concise and accessible form the series provides professionals with a general understanding and a first practical approach to latest developments in business strategy, leadership, operations, HR management, innovation and technology management, marketing or digitalization. Students of business administration or management will also benefit from these practical guides for their future occupation/careers.

These Guides suit the needs of today's fast reader.

Cordelia Friesendorf • Navid J. Mir Haschemi

Private Equity in Germany

Venture Capital for Digital Platform Start-ups

Springer

Cordelia Friesendorf
SRH Hamburg
Hamburg, Germany

Navid J. Mir Haschemi
Unternehmer-Schmiede GmbH
Hamburg, Germany

ISSN 2731-4758 ISSN 2731-4766 (electronic)
Business Guides on the Go
ISBN 978-3-031-33707-9 ISBN 978-3-031-33708-6 (eBook)
https://doi.org/10.1007/978-3-031-33708-6

This Springer imprint is published by the registered company Springer Nature Switzerland AG
The registered company address is: Gewerbestrasse 11, 6330 Cham, Switzerland

Book Abstract

Young, non-conventional businesses that enter established markets with unique products and services are known as start-ups. They are often viewed as displacing incumbents by promoting innovation and changing the perception of customers. In the process of setting up a start-up, start-up founders encounter a number of challenges that can adversely impact the company's long-term survival and success. Start-ups often struggle to sustain their entrepreneurial growth without the help of external funds, despite their reliance on in-house resources. Start-ups are constantly looking for non-debt alternative financing solutions when they are unable to access conventional financing. An ideal alternative to debt is private equity (PE), a form of alternative finance that is widely regarded as a credible alternative form of finance. Digital transformation is causing entrepreneurs across all sectors of business and private life to establish digital platform startups that rely heavily on steady and consistent funding. This is in order to continue operating. In recent years, Silicon Valley was able to build successful digital platforms, which demonstrate the credibility of venture capital (VC) as a source of off-market equity funding. Does Germany have the capability to replicate this kind of success? How do PE and VC investors decide what criteria they will be focusing on when investing in the start-up of a digital platform in Germany? Is there any advice that entrepreneurs should follow when it comes to preparing for VC funding? In order for them to achieve their goals, what strategies should they adopt? It is our goal in this book to explore these questions as well as provide a comprehensive analysis of the ecosystems of start-ups, digital platforms, PE, VC, and regulation in Germany. Our goal is to help entrepreneurs, investors, mergers and acquisitions experts, regulators, and policymakers understand the market's workings and pain points so that they can contribute to the creation of a German start-up ecosystem that is as functional as equivalent organized industries and services, and that has the potential to grow.

Contents

About the Authors

Cordelia Friesendorf is the Academic Director and Professor of International Business Administration at the University of Applied Sciences SRH in Hamburg, Germany. In addition to teaching and conducting research, she consults on corporate strategy, sustainability reporting, digital transformation, governance, and technology leadership. As a C-suite executive responsible for strategic planning and transformation within multinational companies, she has worked in both European and Asian markets over the past two decades and has vast experience in the establishment of profitable business divisions, talent management, and business model innovation. Her experience includes authorship, keynote speeches, coaching, and guest lectures at prestigious universities and business schools. This includes Hamburg University of Applied Sciences, Toulouse Business School, Groupe Sup de La Rochelle, and Haaga Helia University, among others. To address complex issues such as the climate crisis or the growing gap between the rich and the poor in today's knowledge-based global economy, Prof. Dr. Friesendorf advocates collaboration and actively engages governments, businesses, and universities.

Navid J. Mir Haschemi completed his Bachelor of Arts in Business Administration with a focus on Marketing Management and International Management at the Fresenius University of Applied Sciences in Hamburg, Germany, in 2017. During and after his bachelor studies, he acquired early insights among others in the areas of employer branding, finance, and startups. In 2022, he graduated with a Master of Science in International Management from the International School of Management in Hamburg and with a Master of Science in Management with Finance from Edinburgh Napier University in Scotland. Since 2022, he has been working as a consultant at Unternehmer-Schmiede GmbH, a boutique consultancy specializing in the digital transformation of companies and teams.

Chapter 1
The Imperative of Private Equity in Start-up Financing in Germany

Private Equity

Private equity refers to the investment of equity capital in private companies. An investor in private equity invests a sum of money, which is referred to as her stake, in a private company with the intention and expectation of increasing the value of her stake over time.

By taking on the role of a shareholder in the organization, the private equity investor plays the role of an external stakeholder within the organization. Private equity investors may be able to exercise influence in the strategic decisions made by the company based on the size of their stake in the company.

1.1 No Equity, No Innovation

There is no doubt that the advancement of digitalization has had an impact on both private and business life, and this will continue to happen in the future. For example, many businesses are now relying on artificial intelligence-based services to improve customer engagement and gain valuable insights from customer data. This can be attributed in large part to the emergence of innovative businesses and platform start-ups, which are exerting a significant influence on several traditional areas of modern society through their digital transformation processes, which in turn are exerting an incredible amount of influence over a number of traditional areas. As Gray Scott, a futurist, once said: "To understand the future of technology, we need to begin with one fundamental truth: Technology is natural."

Kaplan and Haenlein (2019) indicate that disruptive business models and concepts are driving structural change within companies and across entire industry sectors. It is these innovators and start-up corporations who are disrupting

C. Friesendorf, N. J. Mir Haschemi, *Private Equity in Germany*, Business Guides on the Go, https://doi.org/10.1007/978-3-031-33708-6_1

established markets according to Schumpeter's theory of creative destruction (Metzger, 2019) and creating new markets in their place. These changes can have a major impact on how markets are structured, creating both winners and losers. Initially, the digital revolution was triggered in the manufacturing and industrial sectors, where it enabled the automation of production processes. While it is true that digital disruptions have had a major impact on established markets, it is not always the case that these changes create new markets in their place.

In some cases, the digital revolution has simply led to the consolidation of existing markets, as a small number of companies have come to dominate the landscape. This has been the case in the retail and entertainment industries, where a handful of companies have come to control a large share of the market. In even traditional sectors like banking and financial services, digitalization has become increasingly important for achieving performance metrics in order to increase the level of efficiency and productivity (Friesendorf & Stern, 2020). For example, in the banking sector, artificial intelligence is being used to identify and address potential fraud, as well as to automate customer service and personalize banking experiences.

This context can be illustrated by the fact that large digital platform companies, such as Airbnb and Uber, are just a few examples of how enterprising founders have used creativity to come up with new business models that use technology as a key variable to enter and disrupt established global markets. As a result of the entry of the new player, i.e., the start-up company, incumbents may need to reevaluate their products and offers in order to stay competitive owing to the change in the market positioning resulting from the entry of the new player, i.e. the founders' efforts. It is not surprising that new entrants into the technology industry, or in simple terms start-ups, have impacted and changed entire business sectors in such a short period of time, covering a wide range of industries, ranging from the accommodation sector, often referred to as the hotel sector, and the transportation sector, which encompasses the basic need for mobility (Friesendorf & Uedelhoven, 2021).

As the concept of digital transformation is described by Kaplan and Haenlein (2019), it is a process in which modern technology is used to develop innovative solutions to conventional problems, as well as the creation of new markets and disruptive innovations as a result of the use of modern technology. Considering recent scientific and practice discussions both worldwide and in Germany, it is becoming increasingly apparent to us that it is necessary for digital start-ups to acquire or even become globally competitive on the line of Airbnb and Uber in order to achieve or at least be considered globally competitive. In order to achieve the goals of high scaling, acquiring a sustainable customer base, and as a result, the growth of their own market share and brand awareness, a suitable and adequate financing package is required. To this end, a well-structured financial plan is essential to ensure success in the long term.

Digital platforms are currently facing a rise in network effects on "winner-takes-all" markets, so it is essential for them to remember that these circumstances and necessities are particularly applicable to them because they operate in a context of network effects, which means that one platform is usually more dominant than all others (Metzger, 2020). As such, it is imperative for digital platforms to stay mindful of the opportunities that network effects present, as the right strategic decisions can help them establish and maintain a competitive edge. It is also noteworthy that, aside from the choice of an economic and entrepreneurial environment in which a start-up will be incorporated, the intrinsic innovation-promoting resources that are integral to the ecosystem will also play a crucial role in the success of the company in establishing its market presence (Deeb, 2019). Digital platform start-ups require an extensive pool of innovative ideas and companies, along with a significant amount of financial capital, in order to be able to scale higher and faster in the context of network effects, so as to reach higher and faster levels of growth.

The fact remains that capital is one of the significant resources that start-ups need in order to be successful, and in addition to the multilayered aspects and activities of the start-up process, capital can also be considered one of the most important sources of funding (Kollmann & Schmidt, 2016). There remains a systematic disadvantage faced by young companies when it comes to debt financing, even though the percentage of start-ups that face difficulties with financing declined from 5 to 12% in 2019 compared to 2018. This is similar to the percentage that occurred in 2018 (Metzger, 2020). When it comes to innovative digital start-ups, capital is one of the most important components of establishing their business, particularly during the early stages of their development. One of the main reasons why start-ups fail is due to a lack of capital, a fact that is substantiated by the fact that a lack of capital accounts for a majority of these failures (Metzger, 2019).

1.2 The Role of Venture Capital

Venture Capital

Venture capital is a kind of investment taken by an external stakeholder in a private company, that is not more than 5 years old, and that is not listed on any stock exchange at the time of the investment.

By definition, the act of investing in shares is to purchase them with the intention of achieving capital gains through the sale of them. In the process of buying a share in the company, the venture capitalist is neither a member of the company's board of directors nor an employee of the company.

Since the global financial crisis began in 2009, the funding difficulties confronting innovative start-ups have intensified to a great extent as a result of the global financial crisis, which has led to a great deal of research into alternative sources of funding for these start-ups. A major finding from the process of searching for alternative financing options was the possibility of private equity (PE) financing; this form of funding has become increasingly relevant in recent years due to the fact that it has become more accessible to businesses (Brown et al., 2019). Venture capital (VC) is without a doubt one of the most important subgroups of private equity investments in the capital market. Venture capital is a subgroup of private equity investments that account for the majority of capital that PE investors provide to the capital market, which is why start-ups must have access to venture capital, despite the fact that their fundamental success is uncertain (OECD, 2015).

This is why venture capital, as a subset of private off-market equity, is one of the most important forms of equity financing for start-up companies during the early stages of the development process, especially for those with high growth potentials and a high level of innovation capability. Consequently, this is a method of financing that is highly suitable for start-up companies that are developing digital platforms, because it fits their cash flow and risk profile much better than other forms of financing, because it is able to accommodate their cash flow and risk profile better than other types of financing (OECD, 2015; Metzger, 2020; Friesendorf & Uedelhoven, 2021).

There is no doubt that it is very important for start-ups, especially those that belong to the digital platform industry, to have access to alternative forms of financing in order to be successful in the long run. Due to this fact, digital platform start-ups should consider the investment criteria used in a financing decision when developing a financing strategy in order to realize off-market equity financing in the German market when developing a financing strategy in order to generate financing in the form of off-market equity.

This is not only true when it comes to preparing a financing strategy, but it should also be true when preparing a business plan. As a result, these criteria should be aligned with both these strategies. When it comes to setting up a business model for a digital platform, VC investors are usually the first source that comes to mind when setting up the business model because digital platform start-ups need capital in the early stages of starting up their business. For this reason, it is of utmost importance for digital platform start-ups in Germany to be aware of the criteria that VC investors use to make their investment decisions, so that they can better prepare themselves in order to have a good chance of being selected for investment by the investors.

1.3 Research Gap in Start-up Financing

There has been a tremendous growth in venture capital (VC) and private equity (PE) sectors over the last two decades, and both sectors have gained a great deal of relevance in the academic and practitioner research communities in recent years. The majority of the research conducted has been focused on identifying problems associated with VC funding and opportunities associated with VC funding that have been substantiated through empirical evidence in the majority of the studies. The results of these empirical studies indicate that more than half (67.80%) are directly or indirectly related to venture capital, whereas 26.80% are directly or indirectly related to private equity (PE). As the business environment continues to evolve in a fast-paced and technologically driven manner, venture capital has become and will continue to be a very important source of funding for a wide range of businesses around the globe.

In addition, it should be noted that most studies focus on the USA in general, as they are largely geographically oriented. It has been observed in some studies that only a small percentage of the data is retrieved from Europe, and that only approximately 1.41% of the data is retrieved from Germany (Tykvová, 2018). Among the most critical topics discussed in the literature is how venture capital investors choose which companies to invest in, the process by which they make their investment decisions. Although there is no doubt that the European VC and PE sectors have also become more relevant in recent research, the bulk of all empirical work still relies mainly on US data, even though the majority of these studies have been conducted in recent years (Tykvová, 2018).

According to the findings of the literature review that we conducted, although there is a substantial amount of academic and practitioner literature on PE and VC, there are numerous crucial topics that are of relevance to founders who are seeking funding outside of the stock market that are rare or insufficiently discussed. Literature also points out limitations and shortcomings that are not addressed.

The literature on VC investment criteria indicates that much attention has been paid to VC's functioning, but very little is known about how investment decision criteria are analyzed and explained both generally and specifically in the context of German start-ups.

In our book, we aim to fill these three gaps in the literature on PE and VC financing: investment criteria considered imperative for a VC investment, VC investment tendencies in German start-ups, and areas of focus of VC funds in German digital start-ups. It is our intention to fill these gaps so that all stakeholders in the German startup ecosystem, which spans a wide range of sectors, will gain a deeper understanding of the motivations and behavior of venture capitalists, particularly those who are interested in digital business models within the German start-up ecosystem, and can utilize this information to their advantage.

1.4 Objectives of the Book

Specifically, the purpose of this book is to provide an answer to the research question: Which criteria should a digital platform start-up meet in order to be able to access equity financing through venture capital (VC) in Germany? As you will discover in this book, there is a lot of information about the start-up ecosystem in Germany, VC activities, as well as off-market equity strategies in Germany. In particular, the book provides insight into the specific investment criteria that venture capitalists apply when making a decision to invest in a start-up digital platform company in Germany as a result of making the decision to invest in a start-up digital platform company. Furthermore, it is a compilation of data and information that guides digital platform start-ups on their motivation and decision-making behaviors, as well as what criteria are needed to receive funding in Germany for their start-ups.

Table 1.1 Research questions

1	Is revenue growth considered a VC was investment criterion when deciding to invest in a digital platform start-up in Germany?
2	Is scalability considered a VC investment criterion when deciding to invest in a digital platform start-up in Germany?
3	Is the founding or management team considered ABC investment criterion when deciding to invest in a digital platform startup in Germany?
4	Is an innovative business idea considered a VC investment criterion when deciding to invest in a digital platform start-up in Germany?
5	Are market characteristics considered ABC investment criterion when deciding to invest in a digital platform startup in Germany?
6	Is having well-known invested investors considered a VC investment criterion when deciding to invest in a digital platform startup in Germany?
7	How relevant is financial data? Is this considered a VC investment criterion when deciding to invest in a digital platform startup in Germany?

It is hoped that this compendium will be helpful in preparing startups for funding rounds and helping them enhance their chances of being selected by venture capital companies in the future.

There are many studies, as mentioned above, in the scientific and practitioner literature reviews, that examine venture capitalist decision-making processes and report on basic investment criteria from the point of view of venture capitalists, as well as how they are influenced by these factors in venture capitalist investment decision-making. A large number of studies examined the development of digital platforms specifically tailored to the needs of start-ups. However, very few, if any, examined Germany as a potential investment destination or focused specifically on the development of digital platforms as a start-up business model as a whole. Therefore, it is logical that as a result of the available information, a conclusion must be drawn concerning the specific research question that is being considered on the basis of the available information.

Therefore, eight hypotheses have been developed in an attempt to provide an answer to the research question (Table 1.1). During the process of developing hypotheses for the next section of the research, a research literature review was used to compile findings from the existing literature that have been analyzed and synthesized to develop general findings about the VC investment criteria. As a result of this study, we want to determine whether or not these criteria are valid as general investment criteria for German digital platform start-ups as well as whether or not they are applicable in all cases. This study seeks to evaluate how these criteria affect VC investment decisions when applied to digital platform start-ups in Germany, as well as how specific criteria affect the decision-making process. The objective of this study is to validate the impact of specific criteria on VC investment decisions through the application of concrete practical insights and the expertise of experts.

It is for this reason that the empirical method concentrates its investigation on the expertise of its subjects as its focal point. This study is intended to verify and substantiate the known results in order to be able to draw conclusions from general investment criteria to the specific investment criteria of VC investors when they decide whether or not to invest in a German digital platform start-up. The purpose of the book is to raise the following questions regarding private equity and venture capital that are shown in the following table. By using primary and secondary research, it then goes on to provide answers based on the findings. We will explain the methods that we have used in the next section, and you will be able to see how they have been applied. Table 1.1 below lists down our research questions.

1.5 Methodological Approach

In the literature, there is a gap regarding the investment criteria used by venture capital (VC) stakeholders, whether they are managers or firms that identify start-ups for the purpose of investment valuation, or both. With this book, we aim to fill this gap in the literature regarding the investment criteria that are used by VC stakeholders in order to determine their investment decisions. It is also the objective of this research to gather information on the investment decision-making behavior and actions of VC and private equity (PE) funds in the German market. This is of particular interest since most of the literature that deals with global-scale investments is focused on the American or predominantly Anglo-Saxon market.

There is a wide range of literature available on the goals, motivations, and other factors that stakeholders consider when evaluating or deciding whether to fund start-up companies and the book begins by analyzing the existing literature in the field. It is our goal to provide a comprehensive overview of these factors in order to help you make better decisions. As we move forward in our discussions, we have the opportunity to shed some light on the structure of start-up companies as well as draw attention to the fact that financing is the primary resource that start-ups rely on if they want to succeed in their endeavors. After reviewing secondary literature and reviewing research available from academics and practitioners, we will provide insights that are relevant to an understanding of the concept from a theoretical point of view. In spite of the importance of intent, we believe it's even more critical to facilitate a successful implementation of the concept in a real-world setting throughout the whole process.

Our goal in the following chapters is to discuss and analyze the topics of start-ups, digital platforms, PE and VC funding, as well as issues that are based on both primary and secondary research in order to provide a structured view of the market. Considering the differences in perception of start-ups in general, we decided to take a closer look at the German market since the market cannot be directly compared to the Anglo-Saxon market. It is necessary for us to decipher our observations from the secondary literature, and our expert interviews, in order to be able to answer our research questions outlined in the table above. In order to provide a foundation for our analysis of venture capital funding in Germany, we conducted a series of interviews that provided an empirical basis for our analysis. A detailed description of the methods that are being used in this book can be found in Chap. 8.

1.6 Plan of the Book

First and foremost, the purpose of this book is to provide a holistic presentation of key topics involved in setting up a start-up in Germany along with guidance on how to make the process as simple and as painless as possible for you. There is a need for us to take into account the complexity of the business models of digital platform start-ups, particularly during the founding phase of their business, as these start-ups are heavily dependent on a steady flow of financial resources in order to sustain their operations. It is our intention to discuss the ways in which the financial consulting markets are developing, and how they are geared toward digital platform start-ups. This will enable us to clarify the characteristics and criteria for obtaining the type of financing we are seeking from the perspective of the founders of these companies.

It has been observed that there is a considerable gap in the literature on Germany as a start-up destination; this book fills that gap by examining the perspectives of private equity and venture capital on the funding of digital platform start-ups, as well as getting stakeholder input about the German start-up market to fill this void. It is pertinent to note that founders, funders, financial institutions, regulators, and scientists could benefit from this contribution if they are able to gain a better understanding of how the market works, the entrepreneurial mindset required, and recommendations that will assist start-ups in creating a stable and reliable financial market.

The first step of this book is to elucidate the relevant theoretical foundations for the subject area. This is followed by a literature review of the pertinent literature to provide a comprehensive overview. The hypotheses will then be tested empirically using interview methods in the following steps. An extensive literature search was conducted in both the American and German languages using a variety of sources, including trade journals and reference books.

Chapter 1 of this book describes the concept of innovation as a way of explaining how technology has transformed businesses in a way that has implications for every aspect of life, from the daily grind to the workplace. Our goal is to discuss the challenges faced by innovative market disruptors, such as start-ups, as well as the implications of their dependence on financing for success, i.e. the difficulties they face. The purpose of this chapter is to provide an overview of the private equity (PE) option of venture capital (VC), as well as to explain why the book has been written and what its purpose is.

In Chap. 2, we discuss the nature and characteristics of start-ups as a business model, both locally and internationally, and elucidate what one may expect if one invests in them. Additionally, we explain the different stages of financing as well as provide a clear and comprehensive overview of the start-up process as well as explain the different stages of financing.

As an interesting variant in Chap. 3, we explore digital platforms in the context of start-ups and present the nature, characteristics, and perceptions of the market as a whole. Four case studies are presented in order to demonstrate the need for sustained financing of start-ups founded in Germany and based on digital platforms, demonstrating different levels of success.

Chapter 4 examines the development of the start-up ecosystem, which is in essence a new approach to the concept of an entrepreneurial ecosystem that has become a necessary and sufficient condition for any start-up to succeed. To enrich the setup of such a system, we proceed to examine and explain a variety of factors that may be relevant to start-up success.

In Chap. 5, private equity is discussed as a source of financing both internationally and in relation to the German market. We discuss the developments so far in Germany, pain points and reasons for failure, as well as giving an outlook for future growth based on stakeholder perception.

In Chap. 6, we will explore how VCs can help startups grow and expand in order to become strong. It is the purpose of Chap. 7 to provide a more detailed description of the differences between private equity financing in its broader sense and venture capital financing, which is a much more recent concept. Here, we provide detailed insights on a variety of investment criteria that are considered both for PE investments and venture capital investments.

In Chap. 8, we provide a detailed description of the research design, as well as a thorough explanation of how there is a better fit between our chosen methodology and the research question. It is also important to note that we present the limitations of our study. This chapter outlines our research questions and hypotheses.

In Chap. 9, we present the results of our overall analysis. Our theoretical and empirical analyses are used to validate the criteria. We provide detailed explanations of these criteria.

In Chap. 10 of this book, we have summarized our work in detail, provided recommendations for developing VC financing strategies, and also suggest research topics for future research to be carried out in order to develop the overall field of start-ups in Germany.

References

Brown, R., Mawson, S., & Rowe, A. (2019). Start-ups, entrepreneurial networks and equity crowdfunding: A processual perspective. *Industrial Marketing Management, 80*, 115–125. https://doi.org/10.1016/j.indmarman.2018.02.003

Deeb, G. (2019, April 4). How to build a startup ecosystem. *Forbes*. https://www.forbes.com/sites/georgedeeb/2019/04/04/how-to-build-a-startup-ecosystem/?sh=7736e70c6130

Friesendorf, C., & Stern, J. (2020). Mangelnde Digitalisierung in der Finanzbranche. In *Digitalisierung des Auslandszahlungsverkehrs. essentials*. Springer. https://doi.org/10.1007/978-3-658-32738-5_1

Friesendorf, C., & Uedelhoven, L. (2021). Digital transformation of global mobility markets. In *Mobility in Germany. Springer briefs in business*. Springer. https://doi.org/10.1007/978-3-030-71849-7_1

Kaplan, A., & Haenlein, M. (2019). Digital transformation and disruption: On big data, blockchain, artificial intelligence, and other things. *Business Horizons, 62*(6), 679–681. https://doi.org/10.1016/j.bushor.2019.07.001

Kollmann, T., & Schmidt, H. (2016). *Germany 4.0: How the digital transformation succeeds [Deutschland 4.0: Wie die Digitale Transformation gelingt]*. Springer.

Metzger, G. (2019). *KfW Start-up Monitor 2019. Start-up activity in Germany stabilizes: Intermediate stop or end of the downward slide? [KfW-Gründungsmonitor 2019. Gründungstätigkeit in Deutschland stabilisiert sich: Zwischenhalt oder Ende der Talfahrt?]*. KfW Bankengruppe. https://www.kfw.de/PDF/Download-Center/Konzernthemen/Research/PDF-Dokumente-Gründungsmonitor/KfW-Gruendungsmonitor-2019.pdf

Metzger, G. (2020). *KfW Start-up Monitor 2020. Start-up activity in Germany in 2019: first increase in 5 years – 2020 in the shadow of the Corona pandemic [KfW-Gründungsmonitor 2020 Gründungstätigkeit in Deutschland 2019: erster Anstieg seit 5 Jahren – 2020 im Schatten der Corona- Pandemie]*. KfW Bankengruppe. https://www.kfw.de/PDF/Download-Center/Konzernthemen/Research/PDF-Dokumente-Gründungsmonitor/KfW-Gruendungsmonitor-2020.pdf

OECD. (2015). *Entrepreneurship at a glance 2015*. OECD Publishing. https://doi.org/10.1787/entrepreneur_aag-2015-en

Tykvová, T. (2018). Venture capital and private equity financing: An overview of recent literature and an agenda for future research. *Journal of Business Economics, 88*(3–4), 325–362. https://doi.org/10.1007/s11573-017-0874-4

Chapter 2
The Nature and Characteristics of Start-ups

2.1 Start-ups Versus Conventional Firms

A start-up company is viewed as a special form of starting a business and as an economic or business entity different from conventional companies. Traditional companies and start-ups are perceived to have diametrically opposite characteristics. In contrast, startups typically include young, high-growth companies with a scalable, innovative business idea, which is why they are called startups (Kollmann et al., 2020).

Start-ups create new products or services using exploratory or experimental methods that do not rely on testing, then develops or remodels the existing product by exploiting the gap in the market, and finally perfections this by spending on product visibility and marketing efforts to commercially exploit on a grandiose scale. This founds on the Schumpeterian S-curve of exponential or scaled up growth.

2.2 Start-up Characteristics

There is a common perception that the term start-up is associated with a temporary organization searching for a scalable, repeatable, and profitable business model (Blank & Dorf, 2012). A particular characteristic of this type of business, namely the start-up, is its ability to play a very important role in the development of national social and economic growth, as well as international competitiveness. Whenever a company launches a new product or service, a new market participant will follow, which is a positive stimulus for competition and a way to drive economic growth so that technological advancement is ensured by making investments in new technologies, as well as ensuring the general functioning of the economy as a whole (Kollmann, 2016).

C. Friesendorf, N. J. Mir Haschemi, *Private Equity in Germany*, Business Guides on the Go, https://doi.org/10.1007/978-3-031-33708-6_2

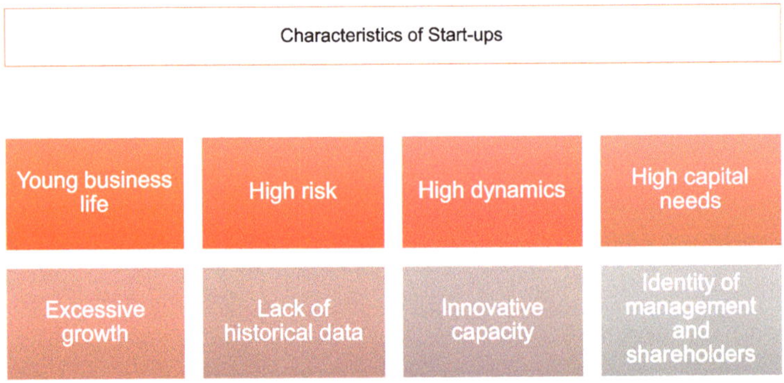

Fig. 2.1 Characteristics of start-ups (Own illustration based on Smeets, 2018)

In addition to causing fundamental changes in industries that have existed for decades on the market and have been established on the market for many years, start-ups also allow for the creation of entirely new markets and the development of innovative business models based on innovative products, services, and processes that will lead to the development of entirely new markets and new business models. In the end, this leads to economic and social progress, as well as the creation of additional jobs as a result (Kollmann & Schmidt, 2016). There is no doubt that the start-up as an entrepreneurial construct has its own raison d'être derived from the fact that other large corporate organizational constructs are hardly capable of bringing technological innovations to the market in sufficient quality and quantity as well as at the necessary speed (Samios & Arnold, 2018). The traditional financial services industry, which includes numerous age-old banks, has seen an explosion of fintech start-ups that combine traditional financial functions with technology to create new products that, for instance, offer easy credit at customer-friendly terms or offer payment schemes that enhance customer loyalty (Friesendorf & Stern, 2020).

In the context of the "German Startup Monitor," start-ups are characterized by three specific characteristics: they are young, they have a technological and/or business model that is extremely innovative, and they are seeking to grow their employee base and revenue by relatively large amounts (Kollmann et al., 2020). Figure 2.1 gives an idea of dominant features of start-ups.

2.3 Financing Start-ups

In general, young start-ups are characterized by having a high capacity for innovation, as well as innovative business ideas that accompany them, as well as high growth potentials and scalability. There are mostly Internet- or technology-related start-ups that are very new to the market and do not yet have a solid foothold on the market (Friesendorf & Uedelhoven, 2021). Furthermore, they are also characterized by a high degree of flexibility, a short life span in terms of both legal and economic terms, as well as a relatively high growth potential. The potential of this opportunity is, however, accompanied by an extremely high degree of entrepreneurial risk as well.

It should be noted that not every business start-up satisfies the characteristics listed above in order to qualify as a start-up company. As a result of the characteristics and innovative characteristics of these young, fast-growing start-ups, it is often necessary for them to obtain large amounts of financing, especially within their first few years, so that they can, for instance, develop products and create conditions for series production. It has been well documented that the typical beginning of a start-up, the beginning of the provision of a service or the production of a good, and the establishment on the market are usually accompanied by a high financial capital requirement, but the majority of the time, founders are unable to fulfill this requirement by using monetary equity alone.

Particularly, due to the exceptionally high entrepreneurial risk and the lack of collateral, there are only a limited number of options, if any, for classic debt financing in this situation. In order to be able to fund their start-ups, start-ups focus on alternative sources of capital as a means of obtaining capital. In addition to this, it is also important to note that potential sources of funding can also be influenced by the stage of development at which the start-up is at and the particular phase in which the young growth company finds itself.

2.4 Life Cycle and Financing Phases of Start-ups

In the literature, different approaches have been developed to categorize young growth companies in further detail. Basically, they can be broken down into different phases based on whether they are development or financing phases. Accordingly, a distinction can be made between the start-up, growth, and maturity phases, on the one hand, and between the development, founding, and growth phases, on the other hand (Smeets, 2018). To secure the start-up's capital needs, a source of financing tailored to each phase and stage of development is necessary depending on the stage and phase of development. As the financing phases change, additional investors with different intentions appear with the different financing phases, enabling different types of financing that are phase-specific. As a result, it can be concluded that there are three major phases of start-up financing: the early stages, growth and/or expansion stages, and the later stages. Figure 2.2 demonstrates the different phases of financing of a start-up.

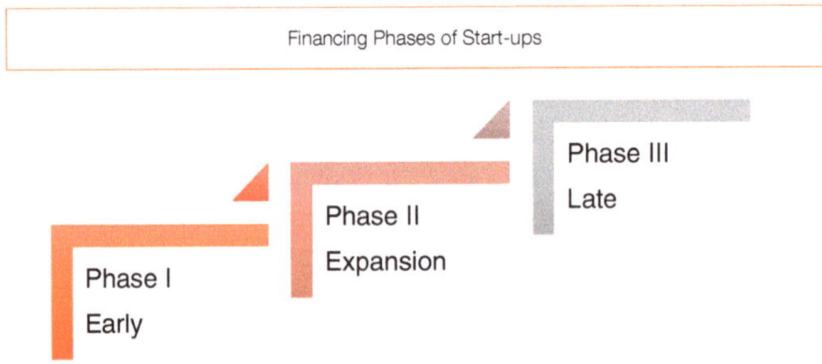

Fig. 2.2 Financing phases of start-ups (Own illustration)

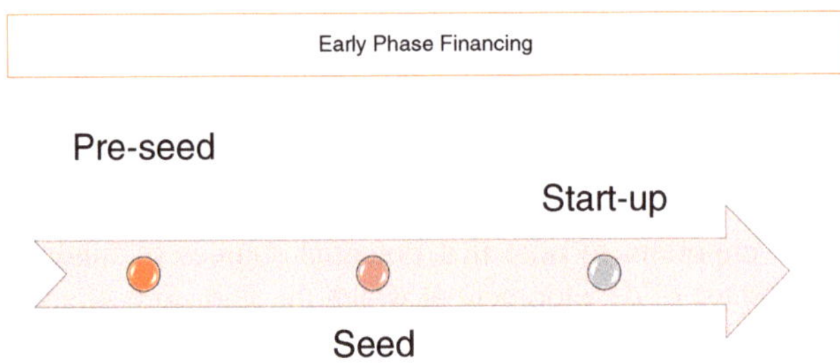

Fig. 2.3 Early phase financing (Own illustration)

2.4.1 Phase I: Early

The early stage can be divided into the pre-seed, seed, and start-up phases. Figure 2.3 gives an idea on the financial needs.

Here, the founders concentrate on generating new ideas and designing a specific business model for the company. As a matter of fact, it is not until the start-up phase that the firm is actually founded. During this early phase, a market launch and the realization of the first positive cash flows may also occur (Vincenti & Winters, 2008). Since capital is already needed in the early phase, this is usually covered by own resources or by family, friends, or acquaintances.

2.4.1.1 Pre-seed

There are several different phases that fall under the seed phase, such as the pre-seed phase, which is essentially a phase of idea generation and the decision to start a company, and it covers the period before a company is actually founded. The seed phase is further subdivided into a subsequent seed phase, which is subdivided into a post-seed phase. Additionally, in addition to the development of the business concept and the business plan, initial considerations are also made regarding the location of the business, the legal form of the business and possible financing options, as the initial investments that are required for the start-up have already been incurred, such as research costs and travel expenses.

2.4.1.2 Seed

As a general rule, the seed phase is characterized by the in-depth development of a positive entrepreneurial concept for the founding of a company and by the development of the business idea into a profitable future business model (Smeets, 2018). It is important to note that the preparations for a foundation begin here prior to the start of operational activities, and that is why startup companies need capital before they can advance their business ideas further. The next phase of development is a period of research investments, leading to the transformation of the mature idea into usable results before it is turned into a prototype (Schefczyk, 2006). Market and customer analyses are also carried out and form the first beginnings regarding the basic development for the conception of the future offer.

2.4.1.3 Start-up

The subsequent start-up phase serves as a means of orienting the company strategically and helps with preparing the company for the start of its operational activities. It is at this point in the process that the activities shift from the formal legal establishment of the company to the launch of a product or service on the market. As part of the strategic business concept, it is further elaborated in terms of marketing, production, and product launch concepts and implemented into a long-term viable business model to be implemented in the future.

Listed here are also the first possible sales successes that a start-up can achieve or track. Since the start-up costs are high, there are low sales revenues and hardly any decisive profits in this phase of the company's growth, searching for financing through new sources of capital or investors is recommended given the sharp rise in capital requirements (Reichle, 2010). In the absence of cash flow returns from the operating business, self-financing is very unlikely to be possible as well. It is usually only the founders' own monetary resources that are sufficient to cover the financing needs up until this stage, and public funding also decreases as the company gets further along, which means that the equity gap could have already been filled by a VC investor at the beginning of the seed phase (Schefczyk, 2006).

2.4.2 Phase II: Expansion

It is during the growth phase that the start-up should concentrate on penetrating its target market and on further developing and expanding distribution channels so that the company can expand its market share (Vincenti & Winters, 2008). It is therefore evident that during this phase, sales volume will increase significantly, but there will also be a decline in product and process innovations as well. In addition to being adapted to the expansion of the company, the structure of the company has also been adapted to match the expansion. This occurs primarily by adjusting organizational and decision-making structures, as well as through increased management personnel. If the high costs and growth investments are financed by cash flow themselves, or if they serve as collateral, it is possible to tap into new sources of financing, such as debt financing, in order to meet the requirements. The feasibility of self-financing is possible once the break-even point has been exceeded.

2.4.3 Phase III: Late

In this regard, start-ups that show above-average growth potential can already start preparing for an IPO as early as the expansion stage of the business or the bridge phase of the business.

2.4.4 Exit

There are several phases involved in the corporate cycle, but the exit is the final phase that represents the conclusion not only from the point of view of financing, but also from the point of view of investor participation. There are a number of other strategies or forms of investment that can be mentioned here from the investor's perspective, such as the initial public offering and the possibility of a buyback (Pott & Pott, 2012). Given the investors' intention to generate profits from their investments, the IPO is the one that is likely to deliver the highest return on investment compared to the other exit strategies, as it represents the most attractive exit strategy.

2.5 Challenges Start-ups Face in Germany

In spite of the fact that the overall start-up rate in Germany has dropped since 2010, as well as emergency start-ups, which is largely due to the improvement in economic conditions and labor market conditions in recent years, there has been a significant increase in start-ups that were founded based on their own intrinsic motivations (Zinke et al., 2018). It has been observed that these opportunity-oriented or market-gap seeking startups tend to be more likely to experience higher levels of innovation and growth potential (Rammer et al., 2016).

Although start-ups are often regarded as "high potentials," the founders of these start-ups are experiencing gradually increasing challenges in sales, customer acquisition, and product development, when considering the German start-up ecosystem (Kollmann et al., 2020) despite the fact that they are widely viewed as "high potentials." The lack of personnel as well as infrastructural capacities and personnel deficits is often identified as challenges for the founding and growth of innovative start-ups, in addition to the cultural hurdles that have long been present (Zinke et al., 2018). Aside from this, aggravating challenges are still being faced in the financial framework conditions, on the one hand, as it pertains to securing liquidity, while on the other hand, as it pertains to raising capital (Kollmann et al., 2020).

2.6 Germany's Start-up Financing Environment

Since 2011, there has been a noticeable increase in the average amount of capital employed by founders. Financing problems, however, remain one of the core challenges that most often cause the failure of start-ups and are therefore considered to be the barrier with the biggest impact on the success or failure of a company, ahead of financial risk (Metzger, 2019). Based on a long-term comparison between 60 and 70% of start-ups since 2008, it has been observed that most of them (based on a long-term comparison, between 60 and 70%) have to bring in financial resources from the outside environment in order to survive.

It has also been observed that since 2009, on average, about half of the founders have mentioned financing difficulties as the main reason for the failure of their start-ups as a reason for the failure of their business. This figure was approximately 57% in 2018 (Metzger, 2019), and the following year, it was over half (54%), according to the same source. There is a continuing barrier or obstacle effect created by the financing issue, so there is a strong barrier or obstacle effect that remains. In spite of this, there has been a significant improvement in the overall financing situation for start-ups in Germany over the past few years. In addition to the conventional challenging aspects for founders, such as the search for talented employees and customers, significantly better conditions have become apparent in financing options. A number of programs and assistance have been established to provide assistance and support, particularly in the early start-up phase, in which low capital is required.

There is no doubt that founded start-ups regularly forecast a financing volume of €2.5–3.5 million in terms of capital requirements for a time horizon of 2 years. However, barely one out of four start-ups can answer the question of where the required capital is sourced. There is still a tremendous amount of difficulty in implementing financing rounds in the one- to two-digit million range, which are primarily used in the growth phase for possible expansion efforts, which continues to be a major challenge in Germany (Van Delden, 2020). An investigation of about 2000 start-ups in Germany found that in the years 2019 and 2020, many start-ups resorted to external funding to raise their capital. This is in comparison with the study of startup capital raised by start-ups in other European countries. In 2019 and 2020, 55.3 and 62.9%, respectively, of start-ups already resorted to external capital, with a continuing upward trend (Kollmann et al., 2020).

A total of €3.8 billion was also raised during this period, which represents an increase of almost €1.7 billion in comparison with 2019 (Kollmann et al., 2020). VC is one of the most important alternative methods of raising capital for start-ups with high growth ambitions and it is increasingly becoming one of the most important sources of financing for start-ups with high growth ambitions. It has also been reported that the percentage of start-ups in the "German Startup Monitor" that are financed by venture capital has risen from 4% in 2019 to 18.6% in 2020 (Kollmann et al., 2020).

2.7 Germany's Off-Market Equity Financing Environment

Considering the recent start-up financing environment, one can say that there is an undersupply, and there exists a high discrepancy between the preferred and used sources of financing, particularly in the German ecosystem. In the context of this undersupply, the most striking fact can be seen in the fact that in 2020, 42.3% of start-ups (around four out of ten start-ups) wanted capital from VC investors, but only 18.6% were able to finance themselves through VCs (Kollmann et al., 2020). According to Kollmann et al. (2019), 39.7% of start-ups want to raise capital from VC investors, however only 14.6% are able to raise funds from VC investors successfully (Kollmann et al., 2019).

Figure 2.4 shows the capital sources that have been used and the capital sources that have been preferred in 2020.

There has been a significant increase in the amount of VC financing in Germany between 2015 and 2019 despite the fact that the actual number of investments was far less pronounced than the desired one—indicating, in principle, an optimistic development of the VC sector (Dealroom, 2020). Innovative and growth-oriented start-ups need the right kind of funding in order to be successful, as they are often denied the necessary funding by traditional lenders. On the other hand, almost twice as many startups (i.e., almost every fifth start-up) sought off-market equity financing to finance their growth in the coming years as compared to last year (Metzger, 2020).

Therefore, the development in the start-up ecosystem in Germany can be described as generally positive, but access to external capital is still one of the biggest challenges facing the ecosystem as a whole (Kollmann et al., 2020). As shown in a 2020 survey of more than 200 start-ups, the majority (74%) of them stated that they would consider it beneficial for Germany as a business location if insurance companies and pension funds were more easily able to invest in venture capital funds. It should be noted, however, that aside from this, 69% of start-ups in Germany are assuming there is not enough venture capital to finance their

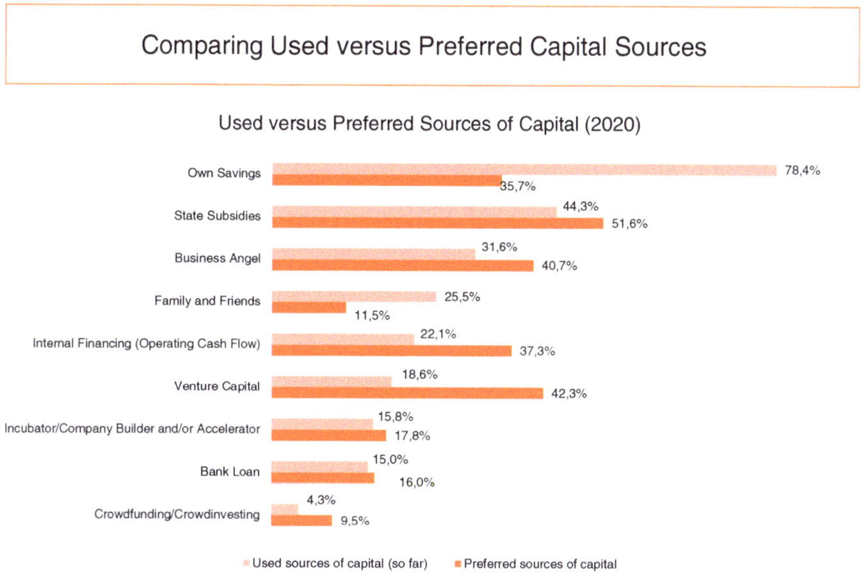

Fig. 2.4 Used versus preferred source of capital (Own illustration based on Kollmann et al., 2020)

businesses, and almost a quarter are considering relocating their companies abroad due to the lack of capital in Germany (Bitkom, 2020).

References

Bitkom. (2020). *Bitkom startup report 2020*. https://www.bitkom.org/sites/default/files/2020-12/bitkom_startup_report_2020.pdf

Blank, S. G., & Dorf, B. (2012). *The startup owner's manual: The step-by-step guide for building a great company*. K&S Ranch.

Dealroom. (2020, March). *Shortage of later stage venture capital in Germany: More acute due to Corona crisis*. https://dealroom.co/uploaded/2020/06/Berlin-Capital-FINAL.pdf

Friesendorf, C., & Stern, J. (2020). Digitaler Wandel des Auslandszahlungsverkehres. In *Digitalisierung des Auslandszahlungsverkehrs. essentials*. Springer. https://doi.org/10.1007/978-3-658-32738-5_3

Friesendorf, C., & Uedelhoven, L. (2021). Digital transformation of global mobility markets. In *Mobility in Germany. Springer briefs in business*. Springer. https://doi.org/10.1007/978-3-030-71849-7_1

Kollmann, T. (2016). *E-entrepreneurship: Foundations of business creation in the digital economy [E-Entrepreneurship: Grundlagen der Unternehmensgründung in der Digitalen Wirtschaft]* (6th ed.). Springer.

Kollmann, T., & Schmidt, H. (2016). *Germany 4.0: How the digital transformation succeeds [Deutschland 4.0: Wie die Digitale Transformation gelingt]*. Springer.

Kollmann, T., Hensellek, S., Jung, P. B., & Kleine-Stegemann, L. (2019). *German startup monitor 2019. More courage, new paths [Deutscher Startup Monitor 2019. Mehr Mut, neue Wege]*.

Deutscher Startup Monitor. https://deutscherstartupmonitor.de/wp-content/uploads/2020/09/dsm_2019.pdf

Kollmann, T., Jung, P. B., Kleine-Stegemann, L., Ataee, J., & De Cruppe, K. (2020). *German start-up monitor 2020. Innovation instead of crisis [Deutscher Startup Monitor 2020. Innovation statt Krise]*. Deutscher Startup Monitor. https://deutscherstartupmonitor.de/wp-content/uploads/2020/09/dsm_2020.pdf

Metzger, G. (2019). *KfW start-up monitor 2019. Start-up activity in Germany stabilizes: Intermediate stop or end of the downward slide? [KfW-Gründungsmonitor 2019. Gründungstätigkeit in Deutschland stabilisiert sich: Zwischenhalt oder Ende der Talfahrt?]*. KfW Bankengruppe. https://www.kfw.de/PDF/Download-Center/Konzernthemen/Research/PDF-Dokumente-Gründungsmonitor/KfW-Gruendungsmonitor-2019.pdf

Metzger, G. (2020). *KfW start-up monitor 2020. Start-up activity in Germany in 2019: First increase in 5 years – 2020 in the shadow of the Corona pandemic [KfW-Gründungsmonitor 2020 Gründungstätigkeit in Deutschland 2019: erster Anstieg seit 5 Jahren – 2020 im Schatten der Corona- Pandemie]*. KfW Bankengruppe. https://www.kfw.de/PDF/Download-Center/Konzernthemen/Research/PDF-Dokumente-Gründungsmonitor/KfW-Gruendungsmonitor-2020.pdf

Pott, O., & Pott, A. (2012). *Entrepreneurship: Setting up a company, entrepreneurial activity and legal aspects [Entrepreneurship: Unternehmensgründung, unternehmerisches Handeln und rechtliche Aspekte]*. Springer.

Rammer, C., Gottschalk, S., Peters, B., Bersch, J., & Erdsiek, D. (2016). *The role of SMEs for research and innovation in Germany: Study commissioned by the Expert Commission on Research and Innovation [Die Rolle von KMU für Forschung und Innovation in Deutschland: Studie im Auftrag der Expertenkommission Forschung und Innovation]* (Vol. 10). Expertenkommission Forschung und Innovation (EFI). https://www.econstor.eu/bitstream/10419/156638/1/StuDIS_2016-10.pdf

Reichle, H. (2010). *Financing decisions for business start-ups under consideration of taxation: A business advantage analysis [Finanzierungsentscheidung bei Existenzgründung unter Berücksichtigung der Besteuerung: Eine betriebswirtschaftliche Vorteilhaftigkeitsanalyse]*. Springer.

Samios, N., & Arnold, A. (2018). *Dealterms.vc: The craft, art and philosophy of venture capital financing for start-ups in Germany [Dealterms.vc: Von Handwerk, Kunst und Philosophie der Venture-Capital-Finanzierung von Startups in Deutschland]*. BoD – Books on Demand.

Schefczyk, M. (2006). *Financing with venture capital and private equity: Basics for investors, financial intermediaries, entrepreneurs and academics [Finanzieren mit Venture Capital und Private Equity: Grundlagen für Investoren, Finanzintermediäre, Unternehmer und Wissenschaftler]* (2nd ed.). Schäffer-Poeschel.

Smeets, M. (2018). *Special features of the valuation of young companies [Besonderheiten bei der Bewertung junger Unternehmen]*. Springer.

Van Delden, C. (2020). Challenges for founders [Herausforderungen für Gründer]. In A. T. Von Hattburg & J. Reiber (Eds.), *Founding with success: Your own start-up company [Gründen mit Erfolg: Das eigene Startup-Unternehmen]* (pp. 3–5). Springer.

Vincenti, A. J., & Winters, S. (2008). The importance of formal venture capital markets in the US and Germany for early-stage financing [Die Bedeutung formeller Risikokapitalmärkte in den USA und in Deutschland für die Frühphasenfinanzierung]. *Finanz-Betrieb, 10*(5), 369–378.

Zinke, G., Ferdinand, J. P., Groß, W., Möring, J. L., Nögel, L., Petzolt, S., Richter, S., Robeck, M. S., & Wessels, J. (2018). *Trends in the start-up support landscape – Incubators, accelerators and others [Trends in der Unterstützungslandschaft von Start-ups – Inkubatoren, Akzeleratoren und andere]*. BMWi. https://www.bmwi.de/Redaktion/DE/Publikationen/Studien/trends-in-der-unterstuetzungslandschaft-von-start-ups.pdf?__blob=publicationFile&v=10

Chapter 3
Digital Platform Start-ups

3.1 Going Digital: An Undeniable Reality

In the context of digitization, we are now seeing the emergence of a new group of young start-ups with digital business models that are highly scalable and digital in nature. One of these types of start-ups is the digital platform start-up, which can take many forms (Metzger, 2020). Economically, the term "platform" can be applied in a number of different ways depending on the context in which it is used. Companies employ platforms as a means of reducing costs by using them to build product platforms within their organizations. As part of value chains, they have also been established for a considerable period of time. The majority of today's popular digital platforms were developed from platforms that already existed in the past. Over the past few years, there has been an increase in the relevance and general preoccupation with platform issues in recent years. Thus, the importance of two-sided markets has grown significantly in the past few years (Baums, 2015).

Rochet and Tirole (2006) were among the first to study these markets intensively. In their study, Rochet and Tirole (2006) described them as markets in which one or more platforms connect two different groups of customers and therefore allow interaction between them. Due to this, the platforms usually court both sides of the connection and charge fees for the services of the connection as a result. In a two-sided market, the transaction volume between users depends primarily on the general structure of the market and not exclusively on the total amount of fees that are charged (Rochet & Tirole, 2006). It has been shown in research that two-sided markets are of particular relevance in the context of general and, above all, economic transformation processes, which has been demonstrated in the rapid growth of digital platform start-ups that are increasingly replacing traditional one-sided markets (Baums, 2015).

C. Friesendorf, N. J. Mir Haschemi, *Private Equity in Germany*, Business Guides on the Go, https://doi.org/10.1007/978-3-031-33708-6_3

3.2 Qualifying Characteristics of Digital Platform Start-ups

As a result of our analysis of several studies on digital platforms, we are confident to say that there are several factors that are common to all of them in defining the concept or idea of a digital platform start-up. It is possible to find a comprehensive review of the definitions in Drewel et al. (2021). Taking a closer look at the definitions, we are of the opinion that they show a series of two essential components: constant core components and variable peripheral components, in the manner proposed by Drewel et al. (2021).

It is evident that both of these components can be found in the intermediate digital platform models that are emerging today. As a result, the operators of a platform establish the necessary infrastructure conditions, as well as the rules of engagement for the interaction within the platform, in which services, products, information, or even currencies are exchanged between at least two interdependent user groups, thus generating added value for at least one of the various user groups (Drewel et al., 2021).

3.3 Drivers of Digital Platform Start-ups

As a result of the inherent benefits of digital platforms, they have experienced rapid growth in recent years. On the one hand, they reduce transaction costs in the sense that they establish a place of exchange between suppliers and buyers, so that transaction costs can be reduced. On the other hand, platforms can also be used as a good foundation for managing innovation in a company. Furthermore, the stabilization and reuse of the central components supports the development of economies of scale and leads to the reduction of costs as well (Baums, 2015). The strongest driver of innovation, however, can be attributed to the network effects that underlie digital platforms, which prevent the entry of individual competitors into the market (Eisenmann et al., 2011). As one of the most significant self-reinforcing factors that has driven the fundamental success and growth of digital platforms, the network effect is responsible for a considerable share of the success and growth of these platforms. A key point of this effect is that it describes how the consumption value of a product changes if the number of consumers of the same product or complementary products changes.

A direct network effect is distinguished from an indirect network effect by making a distinction between the two. According to Katz and Shapiro (1986), the direct network effect states that a product's value varies based on the number of people who consume the product as well as the amount of money that they spend on it. When compared to the direct network effect, the indirect network effect tends to occur when the value of one product changes as soon as the number of users of another product changes, without there being any direct relationship between the products themselves. Two-sided or multisided markets are more likely to exhibit the indirect network effect because they have a two-sided or multisided nature. An increased number of participants on one side of the market also leads to an increased number of participants on the other side of the market and is considered the driving force of digital platforms.

As a result, digital platforms are largely benefited by positive network effects. This is because the more users a platform has, the more appealing it becomes for additional users, so the more users a platform has, the more success it has. As a result of this effect, however, in a competitive environment, only a limited number of platforms can co-exist economically with one another for each market (Drewel et al., 2021). Digital platform start-ups have a particular advantage, as a result of the network effects, when it comes to rapid growth and this is crucial for their success in the initial phase.

The growth of a start-up can also have a greater impact on the valuation of the company than its fully developed business model. Platforms usually grow so rapidly that the possibilities of monetization are not fully clear in advance before they begin to grow so quickly (Baums, 2015). The success of digital platforms would also be determined by the ecosystem in which they are embedded, rather than by the internal resources of the companies that implement them (Drewel et al., 2021; Friesendorf & Uedelhoven, 2021).

The concept of the platform ecosystem is particularly important since it describes the economic mechanisms behind the digital platform models as well as the stakeholders and the interconnected network of relationships that make up the ecosystem (Engels et al., 2017). Stakeholders in this case can be defined as individual individuals, companies, institutions, and other environmental factors that exert an influence on the values created by the platform by exerting their influence on the values created by the platform (Drewel et al., 2021). There are also some already proven principles that can be applied to the development of a successful digital platform, including acquiring customers to convince them of the advantages of participating in a digital platform, facilitating a high-quality transaction process between platform participants, as well as monetizing the platform to ensure a sustainable competitive advantage (Drewel et al., 2021).

3.4 Digital Platform Trends

As a result of the initial disruptive impact of platform models in the business-to-consumer sector, this industry has been significantly reshaped. Several innovative American platform companies, such as Airbnb and Uber, have shaken the competitive landscape in their respective industries with their innovative business models as well as brought about radical changes that have enabled them to take control after dislodging the established dominant companies (Drewel et al., 2019). As a result of the rise of digital platforms, we have seen a drastic change in the structure of industries in a very short period of time. A trend that has been growing for some time now has been for globally leading companies to expand beyond their core businesses in order to create their own platforms to support their growth.

Similarly, the business-to-business sector is also being pushed towards the platform economy in an increasing manner. It is obvious that established companies or incumbents in a wide range of industries are facing increasing pressures because of the disruptive potential of digital platforms (Friesendorf & Uedelhoven, 2021). It is important to keep in mind, however, that they have the additional pressure of already established digital platform start-ups that are positioned in these segments and have specialized in digital platform models through the development of their own platform solutions, as well as the service solutions that they offer (Drewel et al., 2021).

The sharing economy has also contributed to the growth of digital platforms in the sharing economy (Friesendorf and Stern, 2020; Sutherland & Jarrahi, 2018). Among the ten most valuable companies based on market capitalization in the year 2018, six of them were platforms. According to Drewel et al. in 1995, all ten pipeline companies were still operating according to Porter's value chain in the pipeline industry (Drewel et al., 2019). The traditional pipeline markets have therefore developed into platform markets that are increasingly dominating the market (Baums, 2015) as an increasing number of traditional pipeline markets have become platform markets.

In terms of disruptive innovations, there is no other area, particularly that which is driven by the main driver of digitalization, that has such a high potential for disruptive processes than digital platforms. There is no doubt that the platform economy applies not only to the business-to-consumer sector, but also to the business-to-business sector in a growing number of cases. However, it is becoming increasingly difficult for companies to determine which of the targeted customer segments is considered to be of the highest potential for the company and which products are suitable for a platform under the circumstances of a promising positioning (Friesendorf and Stern, 2020; Wortmann et al., 2020).

3.5 Digital Platform Start-ups: Four Cases

The following section presents a total of four different digital platform start-ups that have been founded in Germany in recent years. Two of them were and are regarded as being big successes in the market, while the other two are regarded as failures that can offer valuable lessons to new entrants into the market in the future.

3.5.1 Wimdu: At the Mercy of a Strong Competitor

In 2018, Rocket Internet, which founded the holiday rental platform Wimdu in 2011, had to announce that it would be ending its entrepreneurial activities on the platform. Despite the fact that the company had previously focused on growth and increased presence in the Scandinavian market, the financial investor Platinum Equity terminated the company's business activities. Already in 2016, the start-up had to take numerous cost-saving measures and lay off many of its employees in order to stay afloat. This was mainly due to the strength of the American competitor Airbnb.

Despite having started with strong financial reserves, and despite the fact that Wimdu has raised over $90 million from investors such as Kinnevik and Rocket Internet since it was established and signed up an estimated 400 employees shortly after its founding, the start-up has been characterized as a failure. At the time, Airbnb had only 40 employees, compared to Wimdu's over 500 employees. Even before the business ended, it was evident that the exponential growth that was expected would not happen (Schlenk et al., 2018) even apart from the financial difficulties that the business encountered.

Furthermore, in addition to the financial problems that had to be overcome, there was also a decline in visitor numbers and a decline in turnover, as well as a reduction in marketing expenditures, as well as the departure of a key partner following the takeover of the start-up, which caused business operations to cease (Hüsing, 2019). Moreover, a merger with another weakening competitor as well as repeated sales did not result in any improvement in the business operations of the company (Schlenk, 2018). Besides the strength of Airbnb, the many changes in ownership have also failed to support the pursuit of the planned growth strategies for the company (Schlenk et al., 2018).

3.5.2 Monoqi: Stagnation and Investor Strife

Another digital platform start-up that has now disappeared from the market is the well-known online platform Monoqi, which offered exclusive designer furniture, as well as technology and accessories on its platform, but has since disappeared from the market. It is estimated that the start-up will have 3.5 million members by the end of 2020, and will collaborate with more than 10,000 designers around the world. As a young company based in Berlin, Monoqi has been experiencing rapid growth in the years since it was founded in 2012. It has become one of the leading design platforms on the German market since it was founded in 2012.

During the last few years, the start-up has been able to attract a growing number of customers from other European countries and has generated revenues of around €24 million in 2017, with approximately 100 employees, resulting in an increase in revenues. Due to the fact that the start-up had not yet reached the point of operating break-even in 2019, it continued to rely on financial inflows from investors to ensure its continued operations (Majunke, 2019). The start-up had to file for insolvency for the first time in February 2018 in addition to that fact. Furthermore, in December 2018, they had to file another petition for insolvency in order to avoid bankruptcy.

As a result of uncertainties in funding commitments, both applications were filed and withdrawn again after a short-term funding commitment had been secured from investors (Majunke, 2019). In the first crisis, the start-up was able to resolve the problem by obtaining funds from an investor. However, only part of the promised investment was paid out, since some targets had not been met by the startup. Additionally, the shareholders promised to invest an additional €3 million as a means of securing the start-up's future.

It was expected that after specific restructuring goals had been achieved, further financial contributions would be forthcoming (Kyriasoglou, 2018). Despite the fact that certain successes were achieved in the context of planned and implemented restructuring measures, such as opening the platform to non-members, it was not possible to ensure sufficient financing for further growth (Majunke, 2019). A Belgian design and lifestyle platform, Decovry, took over the start-up in 2020 to become a design and lifestyle platform (Musgrove, 2020).

3.5.3 *Omio: Exponential Growth as a Financing Magnet*

A leading travel platform founded in Berlin in 2013 is Omio, one of the newest German start-ups in the digital platform sector (Petereit, 2020). As a meta-search engine in the early days of the platform, the user was able to compare flight, train, and bus connections in 15 countries and book them directly by using the platform. According to its own data, as of 2019 (Ermisch, 2019), this start-up already boasted 27 million monthly users as per its own information (Ermisch, 2019). With the assistance of over 800 transport companies who act as partners in the platform, customers are provided with a full overview of the connections, the cost of the dependent transport, the travel time, and the combinable partial routes available to them. The idea came to fruition mainly as a result of an extensive analysis of the market and a comprehensive mapping of the market. As a prerequisite for this to happen, the company had to build a critical mass of providers in a highly fragmented market in which there are many transport companies, bringing them onto its own platform (Hajek, 2018).

As far as international expansion is concerned, the USA and Canada are two of the most important markets for the company. It is estimated that 2.7 million users were already registered on these markets even before the entry of the brand (Ksienrzyk & Scherkamp, 2020). One of the most unique selling points of this offer, which makes it stand out from other providers, is the direct booking of the selected offer up to the issuance of a mobile ticket on a smartphone, as opposed to other competitors. There is a single point of contact for the user to receive the service, despite the fact that the actual transport service providers provide the service in the background (Petereit, 2020). In the event that a ticket is bought on a start-up's own platform, a commission will be generated for the company from the transport partners (Ermisch, 2019). It should be noted that the start-up generates commissions not only from ticket sales, but also from services such as accommodation (Hajek, 2018).

Having previously secured a financing of $70 million in 2016, the company was able to record another successful financing of $150 million in October 2018 after a financing of $70 million in 2016 (Hajek, 2018). In this context, Omio counts as one of the potential German unicorns and can boast a company valuation of more than 1 billion dollars (Ermisch, 2019), making it one of Germany's potential unicorns (Ermisch, 2019). The company was also able to secure $100 million in capital from existing and new investors in 2020, including Temasek, Kinnevik, and Kleiner Perkins. Due to the additional funding, OMIO will continue to focus on its vision of making global travel as easy and convenient for its customers as possible.

The start-up is also attempting to establish itself as one of the first globally functioning systems to book transportation services in one place (Ermisch, 2019) and as such tries to establish itself as a leading service. Specifically, the funds will be used to finance organic growth and the potential acquisition of complementary businesses in order to expand the unique product and service offerings of Omio. As early as this year, Omio acquired a competitor from Australia, allowing Omio to grow by 18 million users, 10 million destinations, and 5000 transport service providers (Petereit, 2020).

3.5.4 *Medwing: The Indispensability of Innovativeness*

Medwing is a German start-up that was founded in Berlin in 2017 with the goal of addressing the shortage of medical professionals in Europe (Liao, 2020). There have been a number of start-ups operating in Germany, France, and the United Kingdom so far. It is the business model of the start-up platform that aims to place skilled nursing staff as full-time or part-time employees, as well as temporary workers, as part of its business model. It is the hybrid concept of digital placement and personal contact that makes the platform start-up stand out among its competitors (Stüber, 2020) that differentiates it from its competitors.

The automatic job matching system ensures that workers are connected with hospitals, nursing homes, and other medical institutions as a result of a matching process. Besides this, there is also a career counseling service available for job seekers who are looking for employment. The Europe-focused start-up has recorded 200,000 registered workers and 2500 partner employers so far. If a start-up is successful in securing a placement with an employer, it receives a commission based on the success of the placement (Liao, 2020). There has been a need to build structures and networks at the start of the company in order to obtain the critical mass that is necessary for the start-up to be perceived and taken seriously as a potential partner in the healthcare system since its founding. Working out the entrepreneurial and technological advantage was also a central matter to assuming a good competitive position (Hüsing, 2020).

According to the latest Series B round of funding announced by the start-up in 2020, the start-up was able to secure €28 million as part of the financing round. One of the investors, Cathay Innovation, was particularly pleased with Medwing's investment because it represented the two types of technological innovation that it seeks in companies: first, Medwing was seen as a driver for the future of work by giving employees more autonomy and freedom, and secondly, the start-up was seen as bringing digitalization to a more traditional sector (Liao, 2020). German startups are utilizing funding to extend their technological lead, develop additional features, and expand their reach internationally (deutsche-startups, 2020; Hüsing, 2020).

3.6 Criterion for Digital Platform Start-up Success in Germany

One of the reasons why the exemplary digital platform start-ups cited in this book failed was the superiority of other platform competitors in a limited market, as well as fundamental financial problems. As a result of a limited growth potential, reduced advertising expenditures, declining user numbers on the platform, and failure to reach strategic goals, the need for additional funding was unable to be met adequately because of a lack of adequate funding. For the success of a digital platform to reach the critical mass of users and bring them to the platform, the development of the necessary structures and networks for financing is crucial, as Omio and Medwing demonstrate with their examples. This will make the platforms appear as established market players and would enable them to reach the critical mass of users.

Additionally, for a business to be successful, it is crucial to have an innovative business model that integrates digitalization into more traditional areas, such as healthcare. There are, however, other factors that are equally important, such as the development of an entrepreneurial and technological edge, and scalability—in this case, international—in addition to competitive positioning. Moreover, the existence of specific unique selling propositions (USPs), in addition to a unique range of products and services, enables or supports the success of digital platform start-ups in Germany, due to several factors (Friesendorf and Stern, 2020).

3.7 Distinction Between Start-ups and Digital Platform Start-ups

Even though, in theory, innovative start-ups are to be regarded as digital platforms, in the context of this book, a distinction is necessary, and this consequently needs to be devoted exclusively to digital platform start-ups. To conduct the empirical study, it is particularly important to have specific success-critical criteria for digital platform start-ups, since they are different from most other types of start-ups in many aspects. Digital platform start-ups require a high level of capital to achieve success due to the network effects and the development of a critical user mass. This means they already have a high capital requirement at the beginning of the entrepreneurial life cycle due to the network effects and the development of a critical user mass.

References

Baums, A. (2015). *Compendium industry 4.0 – How digital platforms are changing the economy – And how policy can shape it [Kompendium Industrie 4.0 - Wie digitale Plattformen die Wirtschaft verändern - und wie die Politik gestalten kann]*. Plattformmaerkte. http://plattform-maerkte.de/wp-content/uploads/2015/10/Kompendium-I40-Analyserahmen.pdf

deutsche-startups. (2020, May 26). *Scandit raises 80 million – Medwing gets 28 million – Smava takes 57 million [Scandit sammelt 80 Millionen ein – Medwing bekommt 28 Millionen – smava holt sich 57 Millionen]*. https://www.deutsche-startups.de/2020/05/26/dealmonitor-26-05-2020/

Drewel, M., Gausemeier, J., Vaßholz, M., & Homburg, N. (2019). Entry into the platform economy [Einstieg in die Plattformökonomie]. In J. Gausemeier, W. Bauer, & R. Dumitrescu (Eds.), *Forecasting and technology planning: 15th symposium on forecasting and technology planning [Vorausschau und Technologieplanung: 15. Symposium fur Vorausschau und Technologieplanung]* (pp. 69–100). Heinz Nixdorf Institut.

Drewel, M., Özcan, L., Koldewey, C., & Gausemeier, J. (2021). Pattern-based development of digital platforms. *Creativity and Innovation Management, 30*(2), 412–430. https://doi.org/10.1111/caim.12415

Eisenmann, T., Parker, G., & Van Alstyne, M. (2011). Platform envelopment. *Strategic Management Journal, 32*(12), 1270–1285. https://doi.org/10.1002/smj.935

Engels, G., Plass, C., & Rammig, F. J. (2017). In G. Engels, C. Plass, & F. J. Rammig (Eds.), *IT platforms for the smart service world: Understanding and fields of action (acatech DISCUSSION) [IT-Plattformen fur die Smart Service Welt: Verständnis und Handlungsfelder (acatech DISKUSSION)]*. Herbert Utz Verlag.

Ermisch, S. (2019, February 14). *GoEuro: Travel portal to take off with a new name [GoEuro: Reiseportal soll mit neuem Namen durchstarten]*. gruender.wiwo.de. https://gruender.wiwo.de/goeuro-reiseportal-soll-mit-neuem-namen-durchstarten/

Friesendorf, C., & Stern, J. (2020). Mangelnde Digitalisierung in der Finanzbranche. In Digitalisierung des Auslandszahlungsverkehrs. essentials. Springer. https://doi.org/10.1007/978-3-658-32738-5_1

Friesendorf, C., & Uedelhoven, L. (2021). Digital transformation of global mobility markets. In *Mobility in Germany. Springer briefs in business*. Springer. https://doi.org/10.1007/978-3-030-71849-7_1

Hajek, S. (2018, October 23). *GoEuro: "Combine all means of transport in real time". [GoEuro: "Alle Verkehrsmittel in Echtzeit kombinieren"]*. wiwo.de. https://www.wiwo.de/technologie/digitale-welt/goeuro-gruender-naren-shaam-alle-verkehrsmittel-in-echtzeit-kombinieren/23217374.html

Hüsing, A. (2019, May 14). *After the exit, Wimdu became a mega-flop [Nach dem Exit entwickelte sich Wimdu zum Megaflop]*. deutsche-startups.de. https://www.deutsche-startups.de/2019/05/14/wimdu-zahlencheck-2017/

Hüsing, A. (2020, July 2). *We have been working under the perception threshold for two years [Wir haben zwei Jahre unter der Wahrnehmungsschwelle gearbeitet]*. deutsche-startups.de. https://www.deutsche-startups.de/2020/07/02/medwing-interview/

Katz, M. L., & Shapiro, C. (1986). Product compatibility choice in a market with technological progress. *Oxford Economic Papers, 38*, 146–165. https://doi.org/10.1093/oxfordjournals.oep.a041761

Ksienrzyk, L., & Scherkamp, H. (2020, April 15). So hard the corona crisis hits travel start-ups [So heftig trifft die Corona-Krise die Reise-Startups]. *Business Insider*. https://www.businessinsider.de/gruenderszene/business/reise-startups-corona-krise/

Kyriasoglou, C. (2018, December 21). *Design start-up Monoqi files for insolvency again [Design-startup Monoqi meldet wieder Insolvenz an]*. manager-magazin.de. https://www.manager-magazin.de/digitales/it/exklusiv-desing-startup-monoqi-meldet-wieder-insolvenz-an-a-1244985.html

Liao, R. (2020, May 26). *Cathay innovation's first investment in Germany is healthcare startup Medwing*. TechCrunch. https://techcrunch.com/2020/05/25/cathay-innovation-investment-in-german-healthcare-medwing/?guccounter=1&guce_referrer=aHR0cHM6Ly93d3cuYnVzaW5lc3NpbnNpZGVyLmRlLw&guce_referrer_sig=AQAAAFUnuwB1jcLc6t6J1qTXhzQR2kKoD61D3Uwb373GfvIZP_bpPZCRYzyl2YcSP80IHhRbtM8aAMzECmmQLToluN6fCghWhrXco8CT_Et6F5hFncxfZjw6NxbQMzKjRvyZxteZYJqOFT5f5fjutvZEfPBKy7K6V9AQ5gvPn0yePITn

Majunke. (2019, March 12). *MONOQI successfully sold [MONOQI erfolgreich verkauft]*. https://deal-advisors.com/monoqi-erfolgreich-verkauft

Metzger, G. (2020). *KfW Venture Capital Study 2020 VC market in Germany: ripe for the next development step [KfW Venture Capital Studie 2020 VC-Markt in Deutschland: Reif für den nächsten Entwicklungsschritt]*. KfW Bankengruppe. https://www.kfw.de/PDF/Download-Center/Konzernthemen/Research/PDF-Dokumente-Studien-und-Materialien/KfW-Venture-Capital-Studie-2020.pdf

Musgrove, A. (2020, January 22). *Belgian platform Decovry buys Monoqi to become Europe's largest online design marketplace*. Tech.eu. https://tech.eu/brief/belgian-platform-decovry-buys-monoqi-to-become-europes-largest-online-design-marketplace/

Petereit, D. (2020, January 17). *Startup: Berlin-based travel app Omio expands to North America [Startup: Berliner travel-app Omio expandiert nach Nordamerika]*. t3n.de. https://t3n.de/news/startup-berliner-travel-app-omio-1242044/

Rochet, J., & Tirole, J. (2006). Two-sided markets: A progress report. *The Rand Journal of Economics, 37*(3), 645–667. https://doi.org/10.1111/j.1756-2171.2006.tb00036.x

Schlenk, C. T. (2018, October 22). Former employees sue Wimdu [Ehemalige Mitarbeiter klagen gegen Wimdu]. *Business Insider*. https://www.businessinsider.de/gruenderszene/business/klage-wimdu-hometogo/

Schlenk, C. T., Penke, M., & Scherkamp, H. (2018, September 27). Wimdu closes down – And lays off more than 100 employees [Wimdu macht dicht – und entlässt Mehr als 100 Mitarbeiter]. *Business Insider*. https://www.businessinsider.de/gruenderszene/business/wimdu-macht-dicht-und-entlaesst-mehr-100-mitarbeiter/

Stüber, J. (2020, June 12). *How the multi-million funded Medwing wants to improve care [Wie das millionenfinanzierte Medwing die Pflege verbessern will]. Business Insider*. https://www.businessinsider.de/gruenderszene/health/medwing-pflege-hr-portraet/

Sutherland, W., & Jarrahi, M. H. (2018). The sharing economy and digital platforms: A review and research agenda. *International Journal of Information Management, 43*, 328–341. https://doi.org/10.1016/j.ijinfomgt.2018.07.004

Wortmann, F., Ellermann, K., Kühn, A., & Dumitrescu, R. (2020). Ideation for digital platforms based on a companies' ecosystem. *Procedia CIRP, 91*, 559–564. https://doi.org/10.1016/j.procir.2020.02.214

Chapter 4
The Emergence of Entrepreneurial Ecosystems

Currently, the primary focus on a company's resources and capabilities is no longer sufficient to explain a company's success today. It is the interactions between the company and the environment that also impact the performance of the company on a daily basis. Different dynamics influence the constitution of the ecosystem as well as the development of the company embedded in it. The regional conditions in which entrepreneurs settle and the degree to which they will be able to develop their own startups are, therefore, to a large extent what decide the degree of their own development (Friesendorf and Uedelhoven, 2021).

It follows that the choice of location plays a crucial role in determining the success of Internet-based start-ups. A start-up's location influences its growth during the early stages, as well as having a lasting influence on subsequent decisions made by the start-up in the future. Among the most well-known entrepreneurial ecosystems in the world is Silicon Valley, which is characterized by a high start-up rate and a number of profitable, world-famous start-ups (Friesendorf and Stern, 2020). In addition to Tel Aviv, London, and Berlin, there are other well-known ecosystems in the world.

4.1 Status Quo of Germany's Entrepreneurial Ecosystem

As shown by the Global Innovation Index, as well as the Science, Technology and Industry Scoreboard of the OECD, Germany was recognized as a leader in innovation in 2015. Entrepreneurship is essential to a location's ability to remain competitive in terms of disruptive innovations, among other things, if it wishes to remain competitive. Germany is very well developed in innovation, but there is a very low level of entrepreneurial awareness and therefore of entrepreneurship in Germany, so the rate of business start-ups is also very low, which is also reflected in the low rate of business start-ups.

C. Friesendorf, N. J. Mir Haschemi, *Private Equity in Germany*, Business Guides on the Go, https://doi.org/10.1007/978-3-031-33708-6_4

In spite of the fact that Germany has only been able to record the highest level of Total early-stage Entrepreneurial Activity (TEA)—the start-up rate in 2019 with 7.6%, Germany still resides at the 28th position among 33 comparable countries with this start-up rate, which is the lowest level among 33 comparable countries. The share of entrepreneurs aged 18–64 in other countries is generally two to five times higher than in Germany. Germany has recently acknowledged that, in macroeconomic terms, start-ups are a central driver of economic growth in the national economy and they are essential to the creation of disruptive innovations in the economy in recent years.

As a result, various programs have been launched in order to promote entrepreneurship through promotion of scholarships, growth initiatives, and follow-up financing initiatives, such as small business loans. In addition to this, the Investitionsbank Berlin (IBB) was able to establish that a new startup was founded in Berlin every 20 h during the period from 2017 to 2018 (IBB, 2017). As the number of startup events and the number of founders are on the rise, it suggests that the start-up ecosystem in Germany, and especially in Berlin, is becoming more professional every day.

4.2 Agglomeration as a Necessary Condition

The German start-up scene is concentrated primarily in a few central conurbations and large cities across the country. Several factors have contributed to Berlin becoming one of the top start-up destinations, including its ideal living conditions and disproportionately high level of quality of life for both founders and employees. Furthermore, the relevance of Berlin as a location is further supported by the fact that several listed global players, such as Delivery Hero, have already established themselves there as well; therefore, Berlin is not only known for Germany and probably even as a representative of the entire European startup scene, but also beyond its borders as the main start-up center in Europe.

This is exacerbated by the increasing immigration of foreign IT professionals. The city's networking and political standing favor circumstances conducive to innovation, as politicians strive to improve public perception and the entrepreneurial framework conditions for start-ups, since founders are demanding an increase in funding and a reduction in administrative barriers; particularly in relation to the immigration of talented professionals. The current economic significance of the start-up culture for Germany as a business location, and for individual metropolitan areas such as Berlin is underpinned by the investments made.

In 2020, a total of €5.272 billion was invested in start-up companies across Europe, of which around €3.059 billion was invested into Berlin alone. It was once again Berlin, as in the previous year, that was able to establish itself as the hotspot location for the German start-up scene in 2020, with 314 funding rounds carried out in the city. 40% of all funding rounds accounted for a nationwide trend, therefore, were carried out in Berlin in 2020. However, Munich, the Rhine-Main region, and Hamburg are also seen as important start-up locations and are known for start-ups in the high-tech, media, and games sectors (E&Y Start-up Barometer, 2020).

There is a disproportionately large number of venture capitalists based in the southern part of Germany, particularly due to high-tech developments and a high number of start-up establishments there as well. As far as the rest of Germany is concerned, the situation is quite different in terms of the professional nature of the start-up ecosystem, as start-up rates there tend to remain at a consistently low level throughout the years.

4.3 Transformation Via Start-up Networks

The networking of the digital start-up scene through social networks, annual events, and associations serves as a catalyst for the transformation of the industry, and is helping to enhance the attractiveness of Germany as a location for innovation and entrepreneurship. It is highly likely that the industry will develop into an ecosystem as a result of the thorough reporting of the most relevant events in the scene as well as the cultivation of contacts as a result of the development of contacts within it. It is through this interaction that a culture of exchanging and refining ideas between stakeholders with different motivations but with common goals in a start-up can be fostered.

Among the additional features of the German entrepreneurial ecosystem is the fact that associations organized as Bundesverbände are also involved in the communication of the goals and happenings within the ecosystem to a wider audience, within the framework and limits of organized lobbying. Having said that, these associations have the intent and objective of advocating on behalf of their members with the intention and purpose of obtaining visibility within other industries, and among the general public, as well as of representing their needs to the government.

The goal of the increase in professionalism is to publicize the desire for institutionalization as a result of the increase in professionalism. The objective is to become perceived by the political machinery as a sector that contributes a substantial amount to Germany's economic growth and employment, and to attract foreign investments and talent in the same manner as other successful start-up destinations like the USA, Israel, or China. This goal is perceived by all participants within the ecosystem as improving the existing frameworks in which start-ups are formed, invested, and developed that further depend on maintaining a low level of regulation while having sufficient constraints in order for an industry to grow in a systematic manner (Friesendorf and Uedelhoven, 2021; Friesendorf and Stern, 2020).

4.4 Inadequacies and Upcoming Challenges

According to Bosma et al., the greatest challenges facing Germany as a business location as it transforms into one of the leading digital technology locations lie primarily in the fact that there are a shortage of skilled workers in the country as well as a low level of education in business and entrepreneurship. There is also a problem with overcoming existing regulations and taxation in the German economy that interferes with the goal of promoting and growing entrepreneurship. On the other hand, these barriers also result in young companies having a hard time getting significant capital investment from internationally active investors because of these barriers. As far as the main challenges are concerned, they are related to the deficiency of entrepreneurial culture in the country and the underrepresentation of minorities in companies such as immigrants. There should also be a reduction of bureaucratic hurdles that should be made possible by the establishment and networking of various digital hubs with one another.

As Germany seeks to replicate the success of Silicon Valley in the USA, which is largely the result of a melting pot of migrant investors, students, and entrepreneurs whose common purpose was to exchange and refine innovative ideas in the geographical region of San Francisco, Germany has found it difficult to replicate that model. There have been multiple programs introduced by the German government in the past to encourage migrant students, researchers, entrepreneurs, and investors. These programs include "Make it in Germany," "Study in Germany," and "Research in Germany." But these programs do not translate into the success required due to cultural and societal adsorption into education, employment, and investment. The environment is generally friendlier to natives as start-up founders, rather than migrants, even when the latter bring in the necessary qualifications and drive. A lack of friendly attitudes not only drives out migrant start-up stakeholders but also results in the brain drain of the native population who are unable to estimate business risk and success in a non-transparent, non-value-oriented environment.

According to a survey conducted by the immigrant network InterNations in the Summer of 2022, nowhere are bureaucracy and digitization problems more frustrating than in Germany. The "Expat Insider" opinion poll ranked Germany last when it came to digital infrastructure, administration, housing, and language. In terms of quality of life, everyday problems, and acclimatization, Germany ranked 42nd out of 52 countries. According to InterNations, Germany has room for improvement across the board. In terms of overall satisfaction among immigrants, Germany scores below average—66% of respondents describe their lives in Germany as satisfactory, compared with 72% worldwide. It is also comparatively difficult to settle in Germany, ranking 46th on making friends, 48th on friendliness, and 50th on hospitality. Although migrant respondents highly ranked job security and work–life balance, 34% complained that their employers did not demand creativity or unconventional thinking (InterNations, 2022). For a start-up ecosystem to be successful, these are the two factors that are most significant.

There is still a significant underrepresentation of women in the start-up ecosystem as compared to their male counterparts. The number of female startup founders in 2021 is estimated to be 17.7% according to several government studies. There is an even more severe imbalance when it comes to women investors. There are significant differences in the accessibility to financing through business angels and venture capital as a result of this. It is well known that these instruments are used much more frequently by men's teams, and that female founders or teams are more likely to encounter reservations concerning start-up concepts from—mostly male—investors about their start-up concepts. In particular, disparities are evident in the amount of funding that is being provided. In contrast to the male founders' teams, 5.2% of the female founders' teams have already received more than 1 million euros. This is in contrast to 27.8% of the male founders' teams.

In addition to women, immigrants with an immigrant background are also underrepresented in the start-up industry, although to a lesser degree than women. The number of women who founded startups accounted for 21.5% in 2021, whereas the number of women in the labor force represented 25.9%. However, migrant startup founders face a unique set of challenges due to a lack of networks and as a result, a lack of capital.

The diversity of startups also includes the diversity of regions. Having a startup as an essential part of a successful business is not something that is exclusively found in metropolitan areas. Rural areas also have considerable potential for entrepreneurship, innovation, and a diversity of ideas, as the federal government has recognized. In addition to this, agglomeration centers are increasingly being developed to promote regional economic growth. Developing these centers is now being undertaken to reduce rural-to-urban migration which exacerbates resource competition and causes inflation.

In response, the federal government is also offering support to start-ups in rural areas and regions with structural weaknesses. As a result, EXIST contributes to regionally balanced innovation performance with favorable working and living conditions throughout Germany. This is part of the overall German funding system for structurally weak regions.

4.5 German Federal Government's Initiatives

In recent years, the Federal and State governments of Germany have become increasingly aware of the nature and characteristics of start-ups. The German government recognizes that start-ups possess innovative capabilities and are ambitious in their marketing and scaling efforts, which is of substantial value since they perceive a greater opportunity to introduce innovation by partnering with start-ups rather than incumbents who are less flexible and agile than their competitors. Germany's government seeks to promote start-up innovation, especially in the fields of manufacturing and health, to advance the country's competitiveness on the global stage.

As a leading player in the European Union and at the national level, Germany has committed itself to achieve the goals of sustainability and digitization. For the German government, both goals should be pursued in tandem to accomplish the larger state goals of macroeconomic growth, job creation, and social welfare. Approximately 75% of Germany's start-ups are dedicated to delivering sustainable and digital products or services, which aligns well with the German government's vision of an innovation-driven economic strategy backed by export-driven growth, which is at the heart of the German government's new economic strategy.

In numerous forums, German politicians and policymakers have expressed their commitment to digital transformation and mitigating the effects of climate change at all levels of government. These forums range from business conferences to community-level meetings. Optimal and effective use of big data is crucial for both climate mitigation and digital transformation. Experts agree that data is the "new gold" and that data mining is a basic need, but they concede that there is a huge gap in data structuring and data interpretation that must be addressed for the data to be used intelligently.

It is possible to accomplish this using various types of technology, such as data collection, structuring, and analytics. Most of these tasks or outputs require artificial intelligence, which is of great interest to a wide range of German stakeholders. It is more of a race between nations that include the USA, China, and others to use these technologies to create companies and value-added products and establish a first mover advantage that helps to secure market space, thereby ensuring economic influence. Consequently, the German government is highly motivated to promote start-up ecosystems and remove obstacles for ensuring a landscape of innovation like Silicon Valley or something more unique to the overall European ideal.

4.5.1 Fostering a Risk-Taking Culture

In Germany, the Federal Government views startups as having a particularly important role to play in business, science, and society as they serve as a fuel for innovation and competition. The startup industry is widely viewed as a harbinger of revolutionary ideas and a primary driver of innovation in stagnant industries. Dynamism, renewal, and transformation are features that the German government recognizes and values, so much so that strengthening and promoting the start-up ecosystem has become one of their top priorities. Germany has announced its ambition to join the "Europe Start-up Nations Alliance," which is supported by the Europe Horizon Program of the European Commission. The goal of this newly-created entity is to remove market fragmentation in Europe so as to make it attractive for foreign businesses to enter and start innovative companies that can contribute to EU growth in product and factor markets.

Despite the fact that the startup ecosystem has evolved, there is still great potential. According to studies conducted by various government agencies, the following observations were made:

Key Observations on the German Start-up Ecosystem

According to a recent survey, two-thirds of startups rated their location as good or very good (2021, up four percentage points from 2020).

In 2020, more than 415,000 people were employed by startups in Germany. The number of jobs could increase to 974,000 by 2030.

In recent years, Germany has attracted more venture capital (VC) than ever before. In 2021, the volume of VC investment was approximately 15 billion euros.

In addition to the government agencies in Germany understanding the potential of start-ups, they are also aware of the barriers that prevent the creation of a supportive ecosystem that allows new innovations to flourish. Many of the same problems that are felt in the factor markets, whether it is the labor market or the capital market, are felt in start-ups as well. In fact, there may even be an exacerbation of these factors in the start-up ecosystem, since it is a brand new field that may be prone to these effects. In order to assist in achieving these goals, the government has identified ten areas where it will provide funding and support. In summary, they are as presented in box below:

Federal Government's Start-up Commitment

Increase the funding available for start-up companies

Create an environment where start-ups are able to attract talent—this means allowing employees to own more of the company

Create an environment that ignites a sense of start-up passion—make start-ups easier and more digital

Ensure that there are more female start-up founders and that start-ups are more diverse

Create a platform for facilitating start-up spin-offs from academic institutions and research organizations

Create a more conducive environment for start-ups focused on public benefits

Assist startup companies in securing public contracts by mobilizing their competencies

Improve the ease of access to data for start-up companies

A key focus of this initiative should be on strengthening real labs—facilitating access for start-ups to these facilities

Start-ups should be placed at the center of all policy decisions

4.5.2 Promoting Venture Capital Ecosystem in Germany

Germany is now home to a world-class ecosystem of investors, business angels, entrepreneurs, and academics. To scale, startups need a large amount of capital, which they cannot yet generate from their own earnings. Considering young companies' high-risk structures, traditional bank financing is scarcely available to them. Thus, venture capital (VC) is of paramount importance.

The German venture capital market has grown significantly in recent years. On an international scale, Germany ranks midway when it comes to VC investments as a percentage of its GDP. Late-stage VC financing rounds are dominated by American and Asian investors. U.S. investors finance 63% of the 20 largest European growth companies, for instance. Germany is concerned this could pose a geopolitical threat to its technological sovereignty, innovative strength, and job security.

With its extensive range of startup financing instruments, the German government already aids businesses in future-oriented fields such as digitization, life sciences, technology development, climate and the environment, and education and social affairs. VC rounds will be supported by easing IPO funding as outlined in the Government's strategy paper (Bundesverband Deutsche Startups e.V., 2021).

In collaboration with private investors, the federal government aims to mobilize more public and private capital. As a result, Germany will become a leading location for venture capital. Whenever public funds are provided, ESG criteria (Environment—environmental impact, Social—employee rights, Governance—governance structures) are expected to be considered. All funding measures must comply with the guiding principle of sustainable development. The goals are also aligned with the goals of the environment and climate change. The goal is to create a platform for the next generation of German SMEs and to support the "hidden champions" of tomorrow.

4.5.3 Zukunftsfond and Zukunfsfinanzierungsfond

The Federal Government of Germany is setting up the Zukunftsfond and Zukunftsfinanzierungsfond with the aim of establishing a fundament for the growth and nurturing of a sustainable start-up ecosystem in Germany. The details are provided here below.

Zukunftsfond: An Overview of the Futures Fund

For an investment period up to 2030, the German government and KfW are allocating a total of 10 billion euros. By partnering with private investors, it aims to mobilize EUR 30 billion in private and public capital for Germany as a venture capital (VC) location during this period.

(continued)

In addition to artificial intelligence (AI), quantum technology, hydrogen, medicine, sustainable mobility, the bioeconomy and circular economy, as well as climate, energy, and environmental technologies, these funds will flow to key innovation and transformation areas to be prioritized in greater detail.

With the Zukunftsfond, start-ups of varying stages of development can receive financing tailored to their specific needs. As a result, a combination of equity, debt, and mezzanine capital has been considered as part of the financing strategy.

Growth Phase Funding Modules of the Zukunftsfond

Wachstumsfond or the Growth Fund Germany is a fund of funds aimed at attracting international investors, especially institutional investors to the German VC market

ERP Special Fund promoted by the European Investment Fund towards the financing of start-ups requiring large volumes of capital

High-Tech Gründerfonds aims to support high business models and founders seeking VC

Late-Phase Financing Modules of the Zukunftsfond

European Tech Champions Initiative supports VC financing for tech start-ups seeking large volumes for the purpose of scalability in the later stages of the company

Deep Tech and Climate Fund open up financing options for companies that combine tech with climate mitigation goals at the mid and late stages

Besides the above, the German government is also looking at various debt instruments and thereby may end up also changing the market characteristics of the so far equity-driven financing market in Germany.

It is of considerable importance that the German government uses the opportunity of establishing a start-up ecosystem as a means of revamping the conservative and highly regulated financial and capital markets within its borders. As with the growth fund, a future finance fund has also been established for the purpose of investing in this type of project. As a result of enacting the Future Financing Act, the German government is making a significant contribution to the efficiency and attractiveness of Germany as a financial center, facilitating the access of start-ups and growth companies to capital markets as well as their ability to raise equity capital.

Several key points have already been agreed upon by the Federal Ministry of Finance and the Federal Ministry of Justice. These will be coordinated with the other ministries involved in the process. Apart from adjusting financial market law and developing company law, the German government is also improving the tax framework. IPO requirements will be reviewed by the German government. Alongside the current national measures, this includes the "Listing Act" (revision to the Listing Directive) announced by the European Commission.

This project aims to improve the conditions for the public listing of companies in the EU and to facilitate capital market access for small and medium-sized enterprises (SMEs). As part of this initiative, the German government will also advocate for the relaxation of the free float (Streubesitz) rule. Moreover, the German government will strive to improve the possibility of raising equity capital, including the approval of dual-class shares and the facilitation of expanding capital volume. In addition, it will be examined whether and how the legal framework for modern forms of transactions can be improved to facilitate IPOs.

References

Bundesverband Deutsche Startups e. V. (Hrsg.). (2021). *"Deutscher Startup Monitor (DSM) 2021"; unter.* https://deutschestartups.org/wp-content/uploads/2021/10/Deutscher-Startup-Monitor_2021.pdf

E&Y Start-up-Barometer. (2020). Startup barometer Germany [Startup-Barometer Deutschland]. E&Y. https://startup.ey.com/wp-content/uploads/2021/01/EY_Startup-Barometer_Januar2021.pdf

Friesendorf, C., & Stern, J. (2020). Mangelnde Digitalisierung in der Finanzbranche. In *Digitalisierung des Auslandszahlungsverkehrs. essentials.* Springer. https://doi.org/10.1007/978-3-658-32738-5_1

Friesendorf, C., & Uedelhoven, L. (2021). Digital transformation of global mobility markets. In *Mobility in Germany. Springer briefs in business.* Springer. https://doi.org/10.1007/978-3-030-71849-7_1

InterNations. (2022). *Expat Insider 2022.* https://cms-internationsgmbh.netdna-ssl.com/cdn/file/cms-media/public/2022-07/Expat-Insider-2022-Survey.pdf

IBB. (2017). Funding bible 2017/2018. The guidebook for companies and start-ups [Förderbibel 2017/2018. Der Ratgeber für Unternehmen und Existenzgründungen]. Investitionsbank Berlin (IBB). https://www.ibb.de/media/dokumente/publikationen/wirtschaft-in-berlin/foerderfibel/foerderfibel.pdf

Chapter 5
Private-Equity as Start-up Financing Source

5.1 Features of Private Equity

Private equity (PE) is widely understood as an investment in the form of equity financing in which direct investments of equity are made in private, unlisted companies (Burth & Reißig-Thust, 2018). In other words, equity investments that are not listed on stock exchanges are considered PE.

As a result, private equity spans a wide range of activities, from venture capital, which invests in companies at a very early stage and will have no revenue, but may have good ideas and technologies, to large buyouts, where the private equity firm acquires the entire company. PE is mostly a non-tradable investment in equity or equity-like securities.

Figure 5.1 provides an idea of the characteristics of private equity (PE).

The expectation that shares of private companies will increase in value with time is common among investors. By providing a non-tradable asset, PE makes this activity more valuable. Since the financial crisis distorted investor sentiment and trust in organized markets, PE has become increasingly popular for creating and preserving wealth. In global financial markets, PE has attracted several hundred billion of dollars and euros as a vital trajectory of economic growth.

For this reason, PE is a highly valued investment instrument among financial institutions, investors, corporate executives, founders, regulators, and policymakers. Essentially, there are two main forms of PE: venture capital (VC) and leveraged buyouts. PE entails the functions of managing liquidity, pricing, control, governance, due diligence, value-adding, alignment of interests, and performance measurement. Managing PE requires the ability to gain bargaining power within an auction process, steer company strategy, create operational excellence, and negotiate the best price when the company is ready to be sold. Thus, PE managers drive the

C. Friesendorf, N. J. Mir Haschemi, *Private Equity in Germany*, Business Guides on the Go, https://doi.org/10.1007/978-3-031-33708-6_5

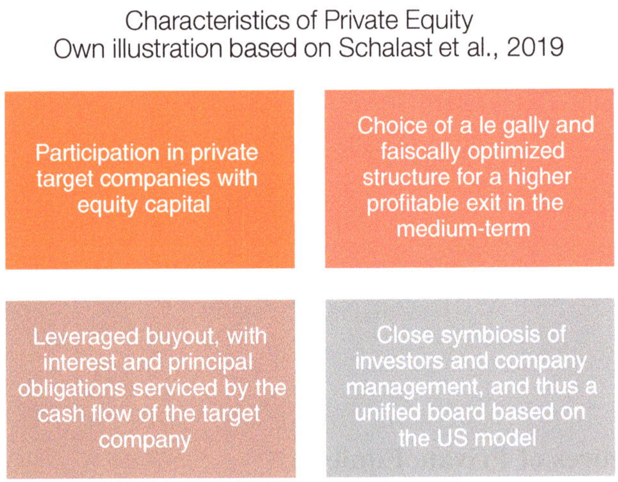

Fig. 5.1 Five characteristics of private equity (Own illustration based on Schalast & Wedell, 2019)

value of their investments to high levels because of their systematic approach, making PE one of the most attractive options in the financial market today. In addition, this implies that the PE manager exerts a significant amount of influence over the board of directors, either alone or in conjunction with other PE investors.

When a PE company raises capital from wealthy individuals and institutional investors, it acquires shares in the company in exchange for off-market equity provided to the start-up for funding (Hahn, 2018). As a result of such participation, the investors have an opportunity to exert decisive strategic influence over the management of the organization within the framework of this participation (Kailer & Weiß, 2018). As far as the investors are concerned, their ultimate objective is to enable the company to surpass the break-even point with the help of the financing—by doing so, they will be able to generate entrepreneurial growth, on the one hand, and increase the value of the business shares, on the other hand.

As a result of the increase in the share price because of the transfer of capital, the shares that are acquired as compensation for the transfer of capital also increase in value as a result of the transfer of capital (Hahn, 2018). In most cases, the desire of the investors to finance the start-up is based on their desire to participate and influence the company temporarily, and they usually exit the company again after 3–8 years (Kailer & Weiß, 2018). Usually, when the enterprise value of the start-up has reached the level anticipated by the investors in advance, it is possible for the start-up to exit and to sell its shares or to recapitalize, with a central focus on maximizing profits.

These types of external financing are typically only available to young innovative start-ups during their growth phase. As a result, they can only take advantage of this type of financing once they have already established themselves on the market based on their own operational business activities and have experienced an increase in demand and turnover resulting from this establishment (Hahn, 2018). Investing in early stages of a company can also be considered PE investment, but most likely falls under the subcategory of venture capital (Burth & Reißig-Thust, 2018).

5.2 Status Quo of Private Equity in Germany

As a relatively innovative asset class, private equity (PE) has very high values, which are greater than average market returns, and therefore, as a relatively innovative asset class, achieves high investor satisfaction during times in which economic conditions make it difficult for investors to generate returns (Burth & Reißig-Thust, 2018). PE is regarded as one of the oldest investment classes, dating back to its origins in the post-second world war period (Fenn et al., 2001) after the end of the second world war. In recent years, institutional investors (such as foundations and insurance companies), as well as wealthy individuals, have been taking advantage of this type of participation in companies to become a more important part of their investment portfolios (Cumming et al., 2013). A significant factor which has prompted this type of financing to be frequently associated with not only admiration and envy but also fear because of the increase in the value of takeovers over the past few decades has been the rise in the value of takeovers.

A study by Groh et al. (2010) on institutional investment in PE over the past few years has revealed that some countries, such as the UK, have shown a certain attractiveness to institutional investors in the PE asset class over the past few years. On the other hand, the attractiveness level of Germany in comparison to the average level of European countries is slightly higher.

It is estimated that there are more than 400 private equity companies working in Germany with a portfolio of around 5500 companies, according to a report by the German Association of Private Equity. A total of 72 billion Euros was invested between 2017 and 2021 because of these investments. As per the report, PE is responsible for the creation of a little more than 1 million jobs and a turnover of more than 200 billion Euros (BVK, 2021a, b). It should be noted that venture capital contributed more to PE than buyouts as well. According to the report, Baden-Württemberg, Bavaria, and Berlin were the regions that received the biggest PE investments, while Schleswig-Holstein and Sachsen received the least investments from the PE sector.

There are several factors that have a significant impact on the attractiveness of an asset class in terms of investor protection and corporate governance rules, as well as the size, liquidity, and condition of the capital markets, which are all important factors to consider (Barber & Goold, 2007). In the German market, particularly after the financial crisis, private equity fundraising and private equity investments have resumed their upward trend following the financial crisis and reached record highs, particularly after the financial crisis. There was a consensus among researchers that this was primarily due to improved market and financing conditions (Burth & Reißig-Thust, 2018).

5.3 Impending and Upcoming Challenges

Despite the steady upward trend in the German market over the last decade, there are numerous challenges for all stakeholders participating herein even though the market is in a favorable position for PE institutions (Burth & Reißig-Thust, 2018). There are several challenges associated with the increased competition in the market, but these are not just about the typical need for differentiation between players, but also about developing specifications for the market. These specifications, for instance, may be expressed in a specific sector and size of the market, as well as in a particular transaction type and other factors.

Further, the development of new transparent, as well as more complex, strategies will be crucial to approach the transformational process of the target objects from a more target-oriented perspective (Bain & Company, 2016). Generally, these new challenges are because of a transformation of the industries, which leads to the transformation of specific business areas, as well as the whole business model itself (Burth & Reißig-Thust, 2018).

A bigger challenge, however, is the boom-and-bust cycles that have already firmly anchored themselves within the industry, which pose the industry with one of its biggest internal challenges. For these cycles to occur, there is an ever-increasing amount of new capital flowing into the industry—and due to the increasing amount of capital coming into the industry, the associated competition for business is constantly pushed forward—which in turn leads to new capital commitments because of high return on investment. Due to the low-interest rates and attractive high returns, there is an abundance of capital, and this, in turn, tends to lead to many higher-valued deals.

In the context of economic crises, the boom-and-bust cycles towards the end of the 1980s and the early 1990s, as well as to some extent the 2008 financial crisis, led to a temporary downturn and collapse during a period of economic turmoil. Several changes took place after the first two waves, including fewer leveraged transactions, higher interest coverage ratios, and more flexible capital structures, along with the industry's own operational competencies. In other words, a strong focus on financial and governance engineering as well as general financial management knowledge, among others, saved the industry from a complete collapse, which in turn propelled it towards the future (Brown et al., 2020).

5.4 The Debate on Regulation

Private equity (PE) will continue to be a significant part of the economy even if significant restrictions and regulations are not adopted in the coming years regarding PE. However, the industry will remain an unstructured industry and will thus remain incomparable to other existing standardized industries in the future. The private equity industry in Germany is experiencing a dynamic growth trend, and this is primarily since private equity investors are constantly striving to improve their key competencies in finance, governance, and operational engineering, as well as consistently applying these skills to their own portfolio companies (Deutscher Bundestag, 2022).

It was anticipated that regulation would have many benefits for the PE sector. Many stakeholders with varying functions agree that it is in the best interest of the PE sector to undergo a fundamental restructuring of traditional business models because of the restructuring. There is also some evidence that a firm that is facing entirely new financial challenges and uncertainty may also be able to receive a clear benefit from introducing regulation in the market as it currently exists. Several companies are also going to benefit from the PE sector's ownership and governance concepts, because the PE sector has steadily gained in attractiveness in terms of CEOs and executives in general in the past few years (Brown et al., 2020).

There is, in principle, a very good selection of investments to be made by PE investors in the traditionally rather strong German small and medium enterprise sector because of the increasing inclination towards international economic standards and the increasingly important issue of succession planning, among other things (Friesendorf and Uedelhoven, 2021; Friesendorf and Stern, 2020). However, a lack of suitable and optimized investment climate hinders the general increase in PE activities, which is why this market is currently primarily driven by the monetary policy of the European Central Bank, one of the world's most powerful central banks (Schalast & Wedell, 2019). According to the research, it can be predicted that the trend of companies remaining private for a longer period, or possibly even forever, is expected to continue (Brown et al., 2020). While this is the case, the German PE market is still seen as one of the most attractive markets in the present time and in the future as well (Burth & Reißig-Thust, 2018).

In response to the developments in the start-up market, the German federal government published its own start-up strategy in 2022 as part of their response to these developments. Taking into account that the challenges that Germany and Europe face are very similar, the German federal government has identified the following measures or areas of action, which are presented here.

Table 5.1 presents a list of the comprehensive start-up strategy measures as envisioned by various state authorities in Germany.

5.5 Private Equity Volume in Germany

It is important to keep in mind that in the context of the German private equity market, in 2019, the share of PE investments in the national gross domestic product was 0.442%, which is an extremely low figure when compared to other European countries. There is a huge difference between this value and the values for countries such as the Baltic States (0.953%), the UK (0.89%), or other immediate neighboring countries (Invest Europe, 2020). Despite this, BVK (2021a) indicates a marked increase in PE investments being made by German PE firms since 2013, regardless

Table 5.1 Comprehensive start-up strategy measures

1.	Strengthen financing for start-ups
2.	Making it easier for start-ups to attract talent—making employee capital participation more attractive
3.	Sparking the start-up spirit—making start-ups easier and more digital
4.	Strengthen female start-up founders and diversity in start-ups
5.	Facilitate start-up spin-offs from science
6.	Improve framework conditions for public benefit start-ups
7.	Mobilize start-up competencies for public procurement
8.	Make it easier for start-ups to access data
9.	Strengthen real laboratories—facilitate access for start-ups
10.	Put start-ups at the center

Source: Start-up Strategie der Bundesregierung, https://dserver.bundestag.de/btd/20/030/2003063.pdf

of where the financing PE firm originates from (BVK, 2021a). According to the BVK (2021a), more than 400 private equity companies were active in the German market in 2020, financing approximately 1000 companies per year.

In the period between 2016 and 2020, a total of €59.6 billion was invested, and more than 5500 portfolio companies with more than a million employees were able to record an annual turnover of €207 billion in the year 2020 (BVK, 2021a). While in 2013, with a volume of only €5.438 billion, investments were made in 1340 companies, but by 2020, investments had been made in 1050 companies, meaning that the total PE investment volume, including venture capital, growth capital, turnaround capital, and buyouts, was €12.554 billion (BVK, 2021a). Most of the PE investments made by German investment companies in 2020 were allocated to Germany, with a share of €7.311 billion (BVK, 2021b), followed by €1.480 billion in Europe, and a small amount of €163 million outside Europe (BVK, 2021b).

There are more than $2.4 trillion in assets under management in 2020, which could be categorized as an asset class since the PE industry is becoming a major asset class over the years. Among the buyouts and growth activities, a majority (more than two-thirds) is accounted for by buyouts and growth activities (Fuchs et al., 2021). A study of the fundraising and financing phases of the German market in the period 2013–2020 also revealed that the industry focused primarily on buyouts and growth/turnaround/replacement capital when it comes to the fundraising and financing phase of the market.

It should be noted, however, that the largest investments made in 2020 were in buyouts and mergers. In the year 2020, a total of 1050 companies were financed, with 12% dedicated to buyouts and 27% devoted to growth/turnaround/replacement capital activities. As for the investment volume, 74% of it was invested in buyouts, and 14% was invested in growth/turnaround/replacement capital projects. The most prominent sources of capital in the fundraising process are pension funds and credit institutions (81% of all capital providers). A majority of the remaining share consists of businesses, family offices, insurance companies, and private and public investors (BVK, 2021a).

References

Bain & Company. (2016). *Global private equity report 2016*. https://media.bain.com/Images/Bain_and_Company_Global_Private_Equity_Report_2016.pdf

Barber, F., & Goold, M. (2007, September). The strategic secret of private equity. *Harvard Business Review, 85*(9), 53–62.

Brown, G., Harris, B., Jenkinson, T., Kaplan, S., & Robinson, D. (2020). Private equity: Accomplishments and challenges. *Journal of Applied Corporate Finance, 32*(3), 8–20. https://doi.org/10.1111/jacf.12415

Burth, B., & Reißig-Thust, S. (2018). Private equity deal success and pre-acquisition determinants – Empirical evidence from Germany. *Applied Economics, 51*(2), 141–154. https://doi.org/10.1080/00036846.2018.1494806

BVK. (2021a). *The German equity capital market 2020 [Der deutsche Beteiligungskapitalmarkt 2020]*. https://www.bvkap.de/sites/default/files/page/20210315_bvk-statistik_2020_vorlaeufig_in_charts_final_0.pdf

BVK. (2021b). *Private equity investments by German-based investment companies in Germany and abroad from 2007 to 2020 [Private Equity-Investitionen von in Deutschland ansässigen Beteiligungsgesellschaften im In- und Ausland von 2007 bis 2020]*. Statista. https://de.statista.com/statistik/daten/studie/12451/umfrage/investitionen-von-beteiligungsgesellschaften-im-in%2D%2Dund-ausland/

Cumming, D., Haß, L. H., & Schweizer, D. (2013). Private equity benchmarks and portfolio optimization. *Journal of Banking & Finance, 37*(9), 3515–3528. https://doi.org/10.1016/j.jbankfin.2013.04.010

Deutscher Bundestag. (2022). *Start-up-Strategie der Bundesregierung*. https://dserver.bundestag.de/btd/20/030/2003063.pdf

Fenn, G. W., Liang, N., & Prowse, S. (2001). The private equity market: An overview. *Financial Markets, Institutions & Instruments, 6*(4), 1–106. https://doi.org/10.1111/1468-0416.00012

Friesendorf, C., & Stern, J. (2020). Mangelnde Digitalisierung in der Finanzbranche. In *Digitalisierung des Auslandszahlungsverkehrs. essentials*. Springer. https://doi.org/10.1007/978-3-658-32738-5_1

Friesendorf, C., & Uedelhoven, L. (2021). Digital transformation of global mobility markets. In *Mobility in Germany. Springer briefs in business*. Springer. https://doi.org/10.1007/978-3-030-71849-7_1

Fuchs, F., Füss, R., Jenkinson, T., & Morkoetter, S. (2021). Winning a deal in private equity: Do educational ties matter? *Journal of Corporate Finance, 66*. https://doi.org/10.1016/j.jcorpfin.2020.101740

Groh, A. P., Von Liechtenstein, H., & Lieser, K. (2010). The european venture capital and private equity country attractiveness indices. *Journal of Corporate Finance, 16*(2), 205–224. https://doi.org/10.2139/ssrn.1307090

Hahn, C. (2018). Emerging growth phase (expansion: Growth financing/bridge financing) [Emerging-Growth-Phase (Expansion: Wachstumsfinanzierung/Bridgefinanzierung)]. In C. Hahn (Ed.), *Financing start-up companies: Practice book for successful founders: Financing, taxation, investor relations [Finanzierung von Start-up-Unternehmen: Praxisbuch für erfolgreiche Gründer: Finanzierung, Besteuerung, Investor Relations]* (2nd ed., pp. 211–333). Springer-Gabler.

Invest Europe. (2020). *Investing in Europe: Private equity activity 2019. Statistics on fundraising, investments & divestments*. https://www.investeurope.eu/media/3052/20200512_invest-europe-investing-in-europe_-private-equity-activity-2019-final.pdf

Kailer, N., & Weiß, G. (2018). *Start-up management compact: From the idea to the business plan [Gründungsmanagement kompakt: Von der Idee zum Businessplan]* (6th ed.). Linde.

Schalast, C., & Wedell, G. (2019). Private equity [Private equity]. In C. Schalast & L. Raettig (Eds.), *Basics of the M&A business: Strategy – Law – Taxes [Grundlagen des M&A-Geschäftes: Strategie - Recht - Steuern]* (2nd ed., pp. 171–205). Springer.

Chapter 6
Venture Capital as Start-up Financing Source

A couple of important things are worth mentioning when it comes to Apple, Amazon, Microsoft, Alphabet (Google), Facebook, Alibaba, and Tencent, which are all among the seven most valuable companies in the world. These companies all have two key things in common: One of the most important reasons why they control the Internet is that they are powerful digital platforms. It is also important to note that they would not have been able to exist and grow as large as they have without venture capital (VC).

These seven companies are all based in the USA, where venture capital has a long tradition of funding startups. Although VC investments in Europe have more than tripled in the last 5 years, Europe still invests 48 billion EUR less than the USA in the same period. Venture capital investment in Germany lags that in the USA. VC investment stakes are catching up on the Asian continent as countries like China and India invest billions of dollars in startups developing future technologies such as artificial intelligence or plainly to set up successful unicorns—these are user-oriented companies that have a minimum valuation of a billion dollars.

6.1 The Beginnings of Venture Capital

The venture capital (VC) industry was established in the 1930s and was only able to grow into a global player through venture capital investment (Sohbi, 2019) that allowed companies to become global players in the computer and technology industries, like eBay and Google, after they were able to obtain venture capital funding (Sohbi, 2019). The term VC has become popular once again with the public mainly due to start-ups like Uber and Airbnb (Becker, 2019). In principle, venture capital (VC) is also private equity (PE), however VC is seen as a more subordinate, special form of equity investment than PE (OECD, 2015). Due to the high loss margins and potential profits of unlisted companies, this type of investment is referred to as venture capital (Börner, 2005; Kailer & Weiß, 2018).

C. Friesendorf, N. J. Mir Haschemi, *Private Equity in Germany*, Business Guides on the Go, https://doi.org/10.1007/978-3-031-33708-6_6

It is noteworthy that there is an extraordinarily high degree of return uncertainty about the capital invested, as most of the time, profits or cash flows are not yet available when the investment is made, since venture capital is typically invested in the pre-founding, start-up, and early development stages of a business (Kollmann, 2005; OECD, 2015). These investments are intended to facilitate a medium-term sale of the shares received from high-risk start-ups or growth companies, usually between 5 and 8 years after they are taken out.

It is important for venture capitalists to evaluate and monitor their investments closely to minimize the high risks associated with investing in start-ups and potential growth companies (Börner, 2005). They also diversify their investment portfolio to minimize these risks. Due to the importance of projected growth and earnings opportunities for an investment decision, venture capital in the current phase of digitalization is primarily directed towards technology-oriented start-ups. Due to the absence of collateral and profits, these startups regularly are unable to obtain debt financing and need capital to close their gap.

6.2 Venture Capital Characteristics

In terms of asset classes, venture capital (VC) falls under the category of private equity (PE). It is common for VC funds to make specific investments at different stages of a start-up company. They can be categorized into three categories: early-stage, growth-stage, and late-stage. A VC investor may act individually or as part of a group of investors. Capital from multiple investors is gathered into portfolios of funds that are invested in newly founded companies known as start-ups that demonstrate a remarkable capacity for growth and therefore are able to attract significant amounts of capital from multiple investors. VC funding typically takes place in several rounds.

VC funding is often motivated by the idea of scaling up the start-up's growth. There are no guarantees associated with start-ups, and as a result, the only option that can offer a value higher than collateral risk is VC. A major principle of VC is that it is based on a high-risk, high-reward philosophy. Even so, venture capital remains one of the most attractive options due to its advantage of investing in another VC firm at the exit stage, or even sell the stake in an initial public offering to another VC firm.

It is important to note that institutional investors, such as banks and insurance companies, operative companies, government funding agencies such as regional or industrial development banks and agencies, as well wealthy individuals, invest in venture capital funds (Friesendorf and Uedelhoven, 2021).

The high failure rate of startups and the uncertainty over the success of growth companies make venture capital investments always relatively risky—hence the term "risk capital" is used to describe venture capital investments. Investing in venture capital is not a high-yield investment, but it is a high-risk investment as well. It is also important to point out that the capital also offers young start-up companies a chance to grow and develop. This is why it is also referred to as "opportunity capital" or "growth capital" because of these characteristics.

6.3 Status Quo of Venture Capital in Germany

It is well known that venture capital (VC) activities are on the rise in Germany since the early 1990s. In spite of the fact that there has been a significant increase in German venture capital start-up financing from 1995 onwards and again since 2012, venture capital activities in Germany have not been able to reach the same level of importance and recognition as they have in the USA, despite a significant increase during the technology boom from 1995 onwards and again from 2012 onwards. Private equity (PE) investors in the USA make significantly more annual investments in VC companies than they do in German VC companies combined with the investments made in PE firms in Germany. After the turn of the millennium, venture capital financing had a hard time in the first few years, mainly due to cheap acquisition loans and PE efforts that flooded the market.

The emergence of a thriving start-up scene in Germany, and, consequently, a German venture capital ecosystem, has been observed in recent years despite unfavorable circumstances. Due to the prominence of a few German Internet entrepreneurs, and because the company-specific future growth and investment efforts of German concerns have a strong focus on digitalization, this is mainly characterized by the prominence of a few German Internet entrepreneurs. As a result of Berlin's constant growth as a European center for Internet entrepreneurs, it has become increasingly attractive for American venture capital funds. As a result, German start-ups have also become increasingly appealing for American venture capital funds in recent years (Sohbi, 2019).

6.4 Expected Venture Capital Growth in Germany

As a matter of fact, venture capital (VC) has been almost exclusively an American phenomenon since the mid-1990s, until a few years ago, and American companies still account for more than half of global VC investments, the situation has changed fundamentally in recent years. At the late stage, it is worth noting that a start-up in the USA would receive at least 10 million dollars of venture capital funding, as opposed to one in Germany that would generally receive under 3.3 million dollars of VC funding at that stage.

It has been reported that the German government does not have a shortage of funds, as per various reports. In 2017, the amount of capital reserves held by pension funds alone is estimated at 7 trillion euros, which is a staggering amount of money. By mobilizing such dormant capital, Germany and Europe could easily fund the innovation cycles that are sorely needed by both regions. Overall, there is much optimism in the German markets in spite of these challenges. A change like this is mainly a result of the rapid and profound globalization, which is also having an effect on venture capital investments and the geographical start-up activities (BVK, 2021b).

The following four future trends can therefore be identified: First, there is expected to be an increase of deals and investments in general in the near future. The second important factor to consider is that globalization will continue to increase, resulting in further global growth for startups and venture capital. Thirdly, the trend towards urbanization also favors the concentration of start-ups and venture capital investments in large cities with global connectivity (Friesendorf and Uedelhoven, 2021; Friesendorf and Stern, 2020). However, this trend will be accompanied by the fourth trend, namely that the most innovative leading companies will be able to differentiate themselves from the competition.

It has been demonstrated that the rapid rise of innovation-friendly cities in Europe and emerging markets is also causing challenges for the American market, as innovative entrepreneurs are now able to obtain successful venture capital funding in their own cities as well (Florida & Hathaway, 2018). VCs will therefore continue to play an important role in financing and promoting innovation in Germany and, in so doing, will promote the growth and development of Germany as a business location in the future (Sohbi, 2019).

6.5 Venture Capital Volume in Germany

In our investigation of fundraising, financing phases, and the largest investments in the German market in the period 2013–2020, we inferred that venture capital (VC) is one of the central areas of the development of the German capital market. Other than the area where buyouts are concerned, the largest investments in 2020 have been made in the field of venture capital. BVK estimates that approximately 61% of the 1050 companies that were financed were funded by venture capital, but of the total investment volume of €12,554 million, only 12% of that amount was invested in VC projects (BVK, 2021a).

In 2020, out of the total VC investments of €1850 million, €109 million were invested in the seed stage, €1273 million were invested in the start-up stage, and €469 million were invested in the later stage (BVK, 2021a). As a result, Germany, which ranks fifth in terms of VC investments as a percentage of gross domestic product, is far behind countries such as Finland (0.120%), the UK (0.107%), and Denmark (0.099%; Invest Europe, 2020) in terms of VC investments.

References

Becker, R. (2019). The business valuation of start-up companies [Die Unternehmensbewertung von Start-up Unternehmen]. In J. Stumpf-Wollersheim & A. Horsch (Eds.), *Forum mergers &*

acquisitions 2019: Contributions from a legal and economic perspective [Forum Mergers & Acquisitions 2019: Beiträge Aus rechts- und wirtschaftswissenschaftlicher Sicht] (pp. 85–102). Springer.

Börner, C. J. (2005). Start-up and growth financing as a financial service [Gründungs- und Wachstumsfinanzierung als Finanzdienstleistung]. In C. J. Börner & D. Grichnik (Eds.), *Entrepreneurial finance: Compendium of start-up and growth financing [Entrepreneurial finance: Kompendium der Gründungs- und Wachstumsfinanzierung]* (pp. 81–101). Physica.

BVK. (2021a). *The German equity capital market 2020 [Der deutsche Beteiligungskapitalmarkt 2020]*. https://www.bvkap.de/sites/default/files/page/20210315_bvk-statistik_2020_vorlaeufig_in_charts_final_0.pdf

BVK. (2021b). *Private equity investments by German-based investment companies in Germany and abroad from 2007 to 2020 [Private Equity-Investitionen von in Deutschland ansässigen Beteiligungsgesellschaften im In- und Ausland von 2007 bis 2020]*. Statista. https://de.statista.com/statistik/daten/studie/12451/umfrage/investitionen-von-beteiligungsgesellschaften-im-in%2D%2Dund-ausland/

Florida, R., & Hathaway, I. (2018). *Rise of the global startup city: The new map of entrepreneurship and venture capital*. Center for American Entrepreneurship. https://startupsusa.org/global-startup-cities/

Friesendorf, C., & Stern, J. (2020). Mangelnde Digitalisierung in der Finanzbranche. In *Digitalisierung des Auslandszahlungsverkehrs. essentials*. Springer. https://doi.org/10.1007/978-3-658-32738-5_1

Friesendorf, C., & Uedelhoven, L. (2021). Digital transformation of global mobility markets. In *Mobility in Germany. Springer briefs in business*. Springer. https://doi.org/10.1007/978-3-030-71849-7_1

Invest Europe. (2020). *Investing in Europe: Private equity activity 2019. Statistics on fundraising, investments & divestments*. https://www.investeurope.eu/media/3052/20200512_invest-europe-investing-in-europe_-private-equity-activity-2019-final.pdf

Kailer, N., & Weiß, G. (2018). *Start-up management compact: From the idea to the business plan [Gründungsmanagement kompakt: Von der Idee zum Businessplan]* (6th ed.). Linde.

Kollmann, T. (2005). Financing young companies in the net economy [Finanzierung von jungen Unternehmen in der Net Economy]. In C. J. Börner & D. Grichnik (Eds.), *Entrepreneurial finance: Compendium of start-up and growth financing [Entrepreneurial finance: Kompendium der Gründungs- und Wachstumsfinanzierung]* (pp. 65–80). Physica.

OECD. (2015). *Entrepreneurship at a glance 2015*. OECD Publishing. https://doi.org/10.1787/entrepreneur_aag-2015-en

Sohbi, H. (2019). Venture capital transactions using the example of first-round financing [Venture-Capital-Transaktionen am Beispiel einer Erstrundenfinanzierung]. In C. Schalast & L. Raettig (Eds.), *Basics of the M&A business: Strategy – Law – Taxes [Grundlagen des M&A-Geschäftes: Strategie - Recht - Steuern]* (2nd ed., pp. 559–576). Springer.

Chapter 7
Venture Capital as a Subset of Private Equity

7.1 Structural Differences Between Private Equity and Venture Capital

There is ambiguity in the definition of private equity (PE), even though it is a term that is widely used. A lot of this can be attributed to the wide range of comparable financial transactions, ranging from venture capital (VC) to leveraged buyouts (LBOs) to mezzanine capital financings that are now available. Developing an accurate outline of the characteristic elements of PE financing is more difficult today than it was 15–20 years ago due to the rapid changes that have taken place as well as the variety of diversifying strategies and focuses developed over the past few years (Schalast & Wedell, 2019).

It is important to note that while there is no clear understanding of the relationship between the terms PE and VC, it is often used in the same context. However, Schalast and Wedell (2019) claim that PE is an umbrella term that should be used correctly, and since VC represents a significant portion of the capital available by PE investors to the financing market, it is also possible to define VC as an investment variant with a unique selling proposition. According to Schalast and Wedell (2019), based on a closer examination, it is also evident that the differentiation of VC investments from other PE investments is particularly justified by the time factor and rather less by any other aspect of their performance.

Furthermore, it is not uncommon for VC financing to come with a minority shareholding as well. PE investors can also acquire minority stakes in a company in the same way as a PE investor can acquire majority stakes in a company. In most cases, VC financing becomes necessary when a young, digitally active company in its early stages is unable to obtain financing from the usual sources of debt capital (such as banks) due to a lack of a good balance sheet history or collateral that would allow the bank to make a loan to the company. Digital start-ups are forced to scale up to be considered internationally competitive, which means that they must rapidly attract many customers, expand their market share, and build up an advantage over

C. Friesendorf, N. J. Mir Haschemi, *Private Equity in Germany*, Business Guides on the Go, https://doi.org/10.1007/978-3-031-33708-6_7

their competitors in terms of brand awareness by establishing an advantage over their competitors. There is a particular need to apply this strategic approach to digital platform approaches since these are often "winner-take-all" markets when network effects are considered.

The costs incurred here are not primarily related to the development and improvement of the product, but rather, to its scaling, so the higher and faster the scaling, the more capital is required (Metzger, 2020c). For a start-up to succeed, capital is therefore essential, and VC investors will provide the required capital as part of the financing provided during the start-up phase. There is, however, no real difference in the attitude towards participation in this case, as it is essentially oriented towards the same considerations and return expectations as a stereotypical financial investor, and, as such, does not really differ from what is expected of the typical financial investor. Therefore, a significant distinction between a venture capital firm and a private equity firm should be made based on how they interact with the start-up over the course of its life cycle and in the context of how they enter the market at different stages of its development maturity.

The distinction between PE and VC is not significant in terms of essential features, even though VC is defined as a subcategory. However, the focus of this work will be on VC in the coming months due to this distinction and in light of the distinction that was previously made between start-ups and digital platform start-ups. Therefore, the investment variant of VC is considered to be separate from that of PE in terms of its differentiation. Due to the fact that digital platform start-ups are generally required to cover a high capital requirement in the initial stage to build up a critical user mass within the framework of network effects, this distinguishes them from VCs. As a result, venture capital is attractive as a source of equity financing because VC investors are able to cover financing gaps at the beginning of a growing company's life cycle.

7.2 Decision-Making Criteria in Private Equity

According to Lerner et al. (2007), there is likely to be a significant difference between the types of investors when it comes to decision-making and investing criteria. As Block et al. (2019) pointed out, there is already an established literature that describes and analyzes specific investor types' characteristics and behavior. However, a wider perspective has yet to be developed (Block et al., 2019).

As part of the realization of off-market equity, it is necessary to clarify in advance which underlying investment criteria play a significant role in the selection and are used as a basis for the actualization of the equity. It is important to note that even though the remainder of this book focuses on venture capital (VC) considering the distinction between private equity (PE) and venture capital (VC), there will also be references to literature on higher-level PE investment criteria in the following sections to help clarify the differences in investment criteria between the two types of financing and to provide a sense of the diversity of investment criteria.

7.2.1 *Stereotypical Target Company Approach*

In the context of a stereotypical perspective on potential target companies and therefore without considering predefined criteria specifications by the investors regarding precise return specifications or regarding the industry as well as the investment focus, private equity (PE) investors primarily seek out potential target companies with sufficient value enhancement potential as part of their investment portfolios. It should be kept in mind that in this unsophisticated view of PE investment, a PE investor would hardly differ from a strategic buyer, so that the only selection criteria for PE investors would be to buy at the lowest price and sell at the highest price.

According to this approach, the PE investor will have to limit himself to this simple selection criterion, because unlike a strategic buyer, a PE investor usually lacks the full complement of value-creation tools that would allow them to realize synergistic benefits, unless there are already potentially corresponding companies within the investor's portfolio, which allows the investor to play a similar role to a strategic buyer in the acquisition process (Schalast & Wedell, 2019).

7.2.2 *Non-stereotypical Basic Targeting Approach*

In general, it must be noted that private equity funds determine their investment cycle based on a number of criteria, such as the transaction size, the sector, the area of activity, and the specific type of private equity (PE) fund (Schalast & Wedell, 2019).

Figure 7.1 captures the investment criteria on PE.

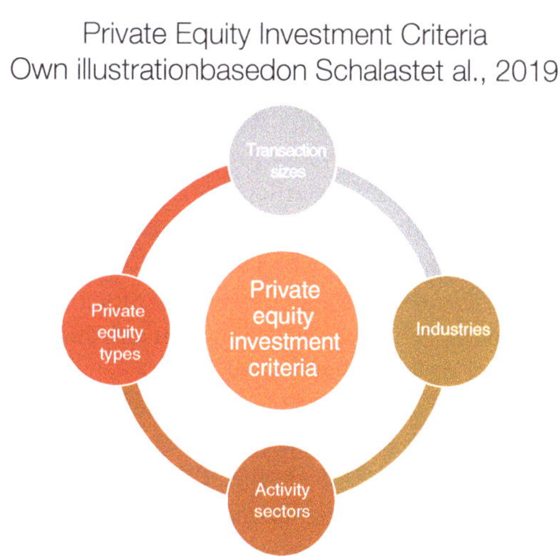

Fig. 7.1 Six private equity investment criteria

Regarding the criterion of private equity (PE) form, although the market remains dominated by traditional buyouts, a variety of PE forms have evolved over the years as the market has evolved. It should be noted that VCs and other project-specific investors, as well as their projects, are increasingly being observed and accepted by the public in general. The size of the transaction can be categorized according to whether it is small (up to €50 million), medium (€50–500 million), or large (above €500 million) and this is particularly influenced by the size of the fund and previous successes of the managers and predecessor funds.

There is however no clear delineation between these two types of funds, as there are funds that pursue a purely national or even global approach to investing as well. Despite the fact that an opportunistic sector selection approach can also be used along with a geographic focus, in most cases, an opportunistic sector selection approach is taken (Schalast & Wedell, 2019). In addition to these criteria, investors are also dependent on the potential for value creation inherent within the target company in order to make an informed decision (Brebeck et al., 2005).

7.2.3 *Target Criteria Before Acquisition*

The general review of a financing decision, especially in the screening and evaluation phases of the process, shows that investors providing equity capital are primarily concerned with minimizing possible risks and failures, such as moral hazard and adverse selection, when it comes to the general review of the financing decision. When it comes to adverse selection, it refers to the decision by an investor to invest in a company, which then fails, or the opportunity that has been missed for an investor to invest in a company, which then succeeds. This concept of moral hazard can be seen as the opportunity for entrepreneurs to change the original project in a way that will result in the project becoming riskier in the future because of their efforts.

To minimize these risks, investors try to reduce the information asymmetry that exists between them and entrepreneurs. As part of the preparation of a business proposal, entrepreneurs will have access to extensive information and data about their own company, its products and services, and the capabilities of their own management and the efficiency of their own business strategies. As opposed to this, investors only have a limited view of these aspects and have only a limited amount of information available to them regarding these aspects. As a result of these evaluations, it is necessary for them to attempt to make an accurate assessment of whether a company will succeed or fail in advance before making any investment decisions (Friesendorf and Stern, 2020).

It is therefore possible for the investor to depend solely on directly observable factors, such as the characteristics of the entrepreneurs, the management team, the characteristics of the product, the characteristics of the market, and the financial data, when making an investment decision and estimating the outcome of the project. An investor basically uses a variety of criteria when analyzing the underlying information about a potential investment object to determine its potential. As investors perceive the investment and company potential through the information available to them, the identification of the most effective criteria for forecasting potential success is the main feature and thereby the key to maximizing the likelihood of a high pre-forecasted return on investment, as the main feature is the identification of the most effective criteria for predicting potential success.

Investors who identify effective criteria and use them in the evaluation process in the context of the general selection problem of successful winners should also find that these criteria lead to an increase in the probability of success in the context of the evaluation process. Consequently, the fundamental analysis of investment criteria is one of the most interesting areas of research for researchers. Even though the topic has been extensively researched in the last few years, Ferrati and Muffatto (2021) contend that there is an extremely fragmented state of knowledge regarding the subject. Most of the older literature has often used a variety of criteria to measure success, but there is a lack of comparability between the results obtained from different studies in many cases (Ferrati & Muffatto, 2021). Among the many studies conducted in the literature, Hamman et al. (2021) discovered that most of them followed the four sub-criteria frameworks developed by Tyebjee and Bruno in 1984: the characteristics of the entrepreneur/management team, the product, the market, and the financial resources.

Hamman et al. (2021) demonstrate in their paper that several criteria investors consider before making an investment decision can be found in the literature, yet they emphasize that not all criteria are of equal importance when making an investment decision (Hamman et al., 2021). On the other hand, Muhammad et al. (2017) applied an adapted version of the individual criteria of personality and experience, as well as company and industry criteria, with the breakdown in product, service, financial and market characteristics based on the product, service, financial and market characteristics.

Additionally, they added institutional and environmental criteria such as environmental risks and country risks to the list of criteria (Muhammad et al., 2017). The validation criteria used by Block et al. (2019) were based on seven criteria in their study. Furthermore, they suggest that despite the extensive literature on the characteristics, as well as behaviors, of certain investor types and the impact of various types of private equity (PE) investments, including LBO funds and venture capital investments, a systematic empirical study of PE investors' investment criteria remains lacking. The research gap in decision-making and investment selection is yet to be filled.

As a result, few studies have examined how PE investors select investments, according to Block et al. (2019). Consequently, empirical evidence regarding the investment criteria of PE investors is limited, since, according to Block et al. (2019), it is difficult to isolate the effects of different company characteristics. There are hardly any meaningful studies on PE decision-making, even though PE investors place great value on their ability to select potentially promising companies.

First, Block et al. (2019) examined the different investment criteria of different investor types. Accordingly, Block et al. (2019) and Gompers et al. (2016) contend that PE investors' specific analyses and measures are fundamentally understudied, even though PE investors devote considerable resources to evaluating and screening potential targets, but ultimately do not participate in many of these. A PE investor screens approximately 15 potential targets intensively, signs an agreement with approximately eight, and closes the deal with only a few (Gompers et al., 2016). Furthermore, Gompers et al. (2016) attempted to partially fill the research gap and provide information regarding the methods used by PE investors in evaluating deals.

7.2.4 *Private Equity Investment Criteria*

According to Block et al. (2019), most private equity investors (PEIs) evaluate companies holistically and evaluate several criteria at the same time when evaluating a company (Block et al. (2019). In the context of screening target characteristics, features from the areas of finance, strategy, management, and company characteristics are primarily considered (Burth and Reißig-Thust, 2018). Through the analysis of 19,474 screening decisions, Block et al. (2019) identified some overarching PE investment criteria in the context of decision-making by different types of PE investors.

The most important factors were revenue growth, the added value of the product/service, and the track record of the management team. Scalability on an international scale, current profitability, the business model, and the reputation of existing investors were also important factors but tended to be of lesser importance (Block et al., 2019).

7.2.4.1 Finance

Lerner et al. (2016) make the argument that PE investors in general tend to focus primarily on companies that are active in growth sectors (Lerner et al., 2016). Block et al. (2019) also demonstrate that growth prospects and therefore sales growth are of central importance in the decision-making process and should therefore be considered two of the most critical investment criteria when making investment decisions. There is no doubt that attractive financial returns are an investment criterion for PE investors, as stated by Dhochak and Sharma (2016).

According to Gompers et al. (2016), equity stimuli play an influential role in the realization of exceptional financial returns and in the run-up to an investment decision by PE investors, as part of the financial engineering that they apply when they acquire portfolio companies. When it comes to financial characteristics, Burth and Reißig-Thust (2018) state that they are mostly determined by key figures such as earnings before interest, taxes, depreciation, and amortization (EBITDA). Therefore, the presence of this value driver is one of the most important factors that influence the decision to invest in PE. As a result of improving the operational performance of a start-up, the investor would be able to increase the EBITDA figures and thereby, be able to negotiate a more favorable deal.

7.2.4.2 Strategy

It has been suggested by Ahammad and Glaister (2013) that the focus in the pre-acquisition phase should be on the strategic areas of a company. Aside from general assets, it is pertinent to note that business models with physical assets, such as machine production, have completely different strategies in terms of customers, long-term goals, and cost structures (Ahammad and Glaister 2013; Burth & Reißig-Thust, 2018). It is also imperative to consider international expansion efforts, as these would be the primary reason for a company to seek or enter into external financing (Friesendorf and Stern, 2020).

7.2.4.3 Management

Block et al. (2019) state that the track record of the previous management team is a central investment criterion for private equity (PE) prior to making an investment decision. This criterion appears immediately following the criterion of the added value of the product/service and even before the criterion of profitability (Block et al., 2019). However, Gompers et al. (2016) found that the leading management team is often replaced by a private equity investor either before or after the investment. Therefore, PE investors look for explicit aspects in the leadership team (Gompers et al., 2016).

Further, Pozen (2007) notes that PE investors are also interested in the fact that the members of the management board hold equity stakes of up to 20%. Gompers et al. (2016) concluded that PE investors offer strong equity incentives to the management teams of their portfolio companies in the context of financial engineering, thereby ensuring management is focused on increasing shareholder value and preventing agency issues. It is important for investors to consider the personality and experience of the entrepreneur when making an investment decision, particularly during the early stages of a company's development (Friesendorf and Uedelhoven, 2021).

7.2.4.4 Product and Service

Hamman et al. (2021) recommend that the main benefit of the product or service that a target company offers should also be taken into account when deciding whether to invest in it. According to Block et al. (2019), the added value of the product or the service is a key investment criterion that comes after the criterion of sales growth and before that of the track record of the management team on the investment decision.

According to Hamman et al. (2021), investors would particularly be attracted to an opportunity if there is a good product or service available, but the target does not have the right marketing channels, therefore offering rapid growth opportunities. In their study, Dhochak and Sharma (2016) confirm that the product or service is one of the most important investment criteria and argue that it is the unique and patented features of the product that could lead to differentiation and give a competitive advantage to the company.

7.2.4.5 Additional Aspects

There is evidence from Burth and Reißig-Thust (2018) that the criteria of ownership by management, age of the target company, and export are hardly statistically significant and are not regarded by investors as relevant criteria in the investment decision process. Also, it seems that EBITDA is not a significant factor in PE investment decisions in Germany, but industry, asset lightness, turnover, and management experience appear to be suitable criteria that can make a significant difference in the investment decisions of PE institutions and influence the success of the deal.

According to Burth and Reißig-Thust (2018), a specific target profile can be developed based on criteria such as these, whereby it can be assumed that companies that exhibit these characteristics are more likely to be able to attract off-market equity financing and to have better performance than those that do not exhibit these characteristics. Therefore, it can be inferred from the inferred findings that early-stage investments or investments in smaller companies are more likely to outperform in the long run than later stage investments. Therefore, companies should actively seek off-market equity financing at an early stage of their life cycle or during expansion planning when it is possible.

Further, Burth and Reißig-Thust (2018) conclude that founders should seek early-stage financing, especially at the beginning, as well as having an executive with management experience who is willing to help with the process. Generally, PE investors would be more likely to seek investment in this stage of the company's development if all criteria for investment are met.

7.2.5 Venture Capital Investment Criteria

It is widely acknowledged that venture capital (VC) investors are among the best studied types of investors in corporate finance, which is why a number of studies have already examined the decision-making process of venture capitalists as well as the factors that influenced their decisions (Block et al., 2019: 330; Dhochak & Sharma, 2016). The selection criteria used by venture capital investors were studied in 1984 by Tyebjee and Bruno (1984). They came up with the following five-stage model for the activities of venture capital investors: initiation of the business, screening, evaluation, structuring of the deal, and post-investment activities.

Furthermore, the researchers also noted in their study that management ability is the most significant investment criterion in the selection process, as it significantly affects both the expected risk and return of an investment (Tyebjee & Bruno, 1984).

Zacharakis and Meyer (1998), however, argue that previous studies that have attempted to contribute to a better understanding of the decision-making process are flawed, which makes it impossible to judge their validity (Zacharakis & Meyer, 1998).

There are some shortcomings to the post hoc methods that are described in Muzyka et al. (1996), but they are generally due to the limitations of the methodology, such as presenting only a limited range of responses to the questions. Using the context of their study, Dhochak and Sharma (2016) show that although VC investors worldwide use different criteria to make investment decisions, specific criteria (such as the characteristics of the entrepreneur, the idea or the product or service, the market characteristics, the management capabilities, as well as financial considerations) tend to be regarded by the majority of VC investors when making investment decisions.

Despite much progress that has been made in the area of VC research over the years, Da Rin et al. (2011) note that further research is still needed in some areas despite the growth of the academic body of work on VC. According to the researchers, one of these areas is the internal workings of venture capital firms as well as the decisions that are made by them as a result. In the first study that compared the basic investment criteria of different types of PE investors, including VC investors, and identified differences between them, Block et al. (2019) were the first to do so.

In terms of investment screening practices, VC investors devote a substantial amount of time and resources to this process (Gompers et al., 2020). When it comes to pre-screening investments, VC returns are primarily determined by the deal sourcing, investment selection, and post-investment value creation carried out by the VC investor. There is, however, no doubt that in principle, all three areas contribute to the creation of value. In accordance with Gompers et al.'s (2020) study, 86% of VC investors rate deal selection as of a high importance and 49% rate it as of the highest importance. Despite the fact that all three areas are essential, deal sourcing and deal selection are fundamentally more relevant than the creation of value after the investment has been made.

In recent years, many VC investment criteria have been considered by several researchers in the context of selecting an investment in the context of selecting a VC fund, according to Ferrati and Muffatto (2021). According to our findings, the most frequently considered criterion classes were the characteristics of the entrepreneur and/or management team, the product or service, and the market, as well as the financial data, of the company. According to Ferrati and Muffatto (2021), this division supports the "jockey versus horse controversy" in investment literature. It is argued that investors make their financing decisions based on the jockey (entrepreneurs and managers), the horse (products/services), the racetrack (market size and growth rate), or the odds (financials).

It has been found that, for the most part, the characteristics of the team were considered a key component in the context of the decision to invest in the studies selected. As Ferrati and Muffatto (2021) point out, while considering the 208 criteria that have been identified so far in the existing literature has enabled a more specific view, and led to a more precise perception, it has also revealed limitations, because the area surrounding the team has been examined far more frequently than the area dealing with the product or the market, according to Ferrati and Muffatto (2021).

Ferrati and Muffatto (2021) raise the question of whether investors are paying more attention to a particular aspect of a business such as a team and less attention to another aspect such as the product or the market. This may be due to the difficulty in identifying general criteria against which specific elements of a company, such as its product or the business model, can be evaluated. This could be explained mainly by the difficulty in identifying general criteria against which specific elements of a company can be evaluated. As a result of the study, it must be noted that previous research has assumed that the team is the most critical investment criterion when it comes to making a decision.

Entrepreneurial ventures, therefore, are considered to be mainly based on the contributions of their founders. According to Zopounidis (1994), despite the fact that the particular criteria, as well as the weighting assigned to them, used in studies vary considerably, most studies done to date have cited specific criteria to which particular importance has been attached, such as market characteristics and the management team. In the meantime, a number of studies, such as that by Block et al. (2019) have demonstrated that VC investment criteria differ significantly from those of other types of private equity (PE) investors.

Consequently, VC investors place a significantly greater emphasis on high sales growth than they do on profitability (Block et al., 2019). Ueda (2004) cited these results as a way of assessing VC investments as fundamentally risky and focused on fast-growth companies. As a result, Puri and Zarutskie (2012) argue that VC investors disproportionately invest in companies without significant commercial revenues in both the high-tech and low-tech industries, and that they tend to focus on the long-term scalability of the company, rather than short-term profitability.

VC investors pay less attention to current profitability than other investor types (such as family offices, growth equity funds, and LBO funds) Block et al. (2019) found that VC investors focus more on scaling potential than other investor types (such as family offices, growth equity funds, and LBO funds). Due to its higher scalability, VC investors are becoming more interested in revenue growth. This is due to the fact that they have to deliver returns to their partners within a relatively short period of time. This is reflected in the increased interest of VC investors in revenue growth. As a result, VC investors tend to make more risky investments as a result.

In addition to this, companies with high profits are not the ideal prerequisites for outperforming other fund managers and thus increasing their own popularity, as apart from the desire to earn a profit, there is also the desire for status and outperforming their competitors as well (Block et al., 2019). There is also a preference among VC investors to invest in companies that have already been backed by well-known investors (Block et al., 2019). The authors of Hsu (2004) cite this criterion as an appropriate one, highlighting that VC funds may be able to charge future entrepreneurs a higher premium for their investment because they will be integrated into better-connected networks as a result of their investment by reputable VC firms.

As a result, companies can expect more opportunities for growth in the future. As a result of establishing an excellent reputation, it would also be easier to source future investments in the future (Megginson & Weiss, 1991). As reported by Hochberg et al. (2007) and Lerner (1994), VC investors who have a larger and more professional network could, in principle, improve the performance of their funds and reduce risk by syndicating deals with other investors. Furthermore, VC investors find that innovation-oriented business models are more likely to be attractive to them, as this is in line with their pursuit of risk-affine strategies, as well as their willingness to trade off high risks for higher returns. Due to this, VC investors also attach increased importance to the high-added-value of the products and services that a company is selling. In their study, Gompers et al. (2020) found that in addition to the business model or the product or service idea, the relevance of the business model also plays a critical role.

It has been demonstrated by Hamman et al. (2021) that results previously derived from other international studies cannot be applied to all locations. According to the researchers, the criteria for making an investment decision are determined by the location of the investment. In view of this, they concluded that there is general uncertainty about which criteria should be considered central when making investment decisions (Metzger, 2019; Metzger, 2020a, b). This is especially true when dealing with challenging circumstances during the same. Block et al.'s more recent study shows that, in principle, one of the most significant investment criteria is the management team. This is because the importance attached to the management team, among other things, does not differ significantly between the different kinds of PE investors. According to the study (2019), one of the most critical investment criteria is the management team, among other things.

Despite this, Block et al. (2019) also found that investors are more interested in the revenue growth of a company and the added value that it provides to the market through its products or services than they are in the management team's track record. There is no doubt that the team is one of the most influential factors for success (96% of respondents) as well as failure (92% of respondents) for VC investors as reported by Gompers et al. (2020). Additionally, it was striking to find that most of the VC investors in the study did not see their own contributions as a cause of success or failure in their venture.

7.2.6 Financial Resource Crunch May Hamper Start-up Growth

In the context of disruptive digital transformation processes, the establishment of digital platform start-ups is increasing and influencing the business activities of various industries. In addition, the literature review demonstrated that the general environment for start-ups, the entrepreneurial ecosystem in Germany, and the financing environment in Germany have improved over the past few years, but that financing remains a significant challenge for start-ups and digital platform companies.

After considering the overarching theme of this thesis in the context of the analysis, thematic delimitations were made. Since digital platform start-ups must build up a critical mass of users at an early stage, they differ from other start-ups. Because digital platform start-ups also have a high capital requirement at an early stage because they must build up a critical mass of users at an early stage.

Therefore, a distinction was also made between private equity (PE) and venture capital (VC). Even though the investment type VC is not significantly different from the superordinate generic term PE, there are some key differences. Based on the time of entry of the investment, there is a significant difference in the context of the work. Digital platform start-ups require financing during the early development phases, and VC investors are therefore primarily considered a source of financing since PE investments are made towards the end of an entrepreneur's life cycle, whereas VC investments are made towards the beginning of the project life cycle. This book treats venture capital as a separate type of investment.

A review of the identifiable literature was conducted to provide an overview of the investment criteria that PE and VC investors consider when making investment decisions. The review of the available literature revealed that the topic is fundamentally associated with a divided state of research and that few meaningful publications exist. In addition, it was difficult to make a general statement regarding the most relevant investment criteria for PE and VC investors. So far, the German market and digital platform start-ups have also been largely ignored.

Although the literature search revealed studies that deal with general investment criteria of VC investors, hardly any study was found regarding specific VC investment criteria used when deciding on an investment in digital platform start-ups. Thus, this empirical study seeks to determine what criteria must be fulfilled by a digital platform startup to obtain equity financing from venture capital in Germany.

References

Ahammad, M. F., & Glaister, K. W. (2013). The pre-acquisition evaluation of target firms and cross border acquisition performance. *International Business Review, 22*, 894–904. https://doi.org/10.2139/ssrn.1549830

Block, J., Fisch, C., Vismara, S., & Andres, R. (2019). Private equity investment criteria: An experimental conjoint analysis of venture capital, business angels, and family offices. *Journal of Corporate Finance, 58*, 329–352. https://doi.org/10.1016/j.jcorpfin.2019.05.009

Brebeck, F., Kothes, W., & Schönbeck, T. (2005). Traditional and innovative company valuation by financial investors [Traditionelle und innovative Unternehmensbewertung durch Finanzinvestoren]. In W. Berens, H. U. Brauner, & J. Frodermann (Eds.), *Company development with financial investors: equity strengthening, value enhancement, company sale [Unternehmensentwicklung mit Finanzinvestoren: Eigenkapitalstärkung, Wertsteigerung, Unternehmensverkauf]* (pp. 87–115). Schäffer-Poeschel.

Burth, B., & Reißig-Thust, S. (2018). Private equity deal success and pre-acquisition determinants – Empirical evidence from Germany. *Applied Economics, 51*(2), 141–154. https://doi.org/10.1080/00036846.2018.1494806

Da Rin, M., Hellmann, T. F., & Puri, M. (2011, October 12). *A survey of venture capital research*. https://doi.org/10.2139/ssrn.1942821.

Dhochak, M., & Sharma, A. K. (2016). Identification and prioritization of factors affecting venture capitalists' investment decision-making process. *Journal of Small Business and Enterprise Development, 23*(4), 964–983. https://doi.org/10.1108/jsbed-12-2015-0166

Ferrati, F., & Muffatto, M. (2021). Reviewing equity investors' funding criteria: A comprehensive classification and research agenda. *Venture Capital. An International Journal of Entrepreneurial Finance, 23*(2), 157–178. https://doi.org/10.1080/13691066.2021.1883211

Friesendorf, C., & Stern, J. (2020). Mangelnde Digitalisierung in der Finanzbranche. In *Digitalisierung des Auslandszahlungsverkehrs. essentials*. Springer. https://doi.org/10.1007/978-3-658-32738-5_1

Friesendorf, C., & Uedelhoven, L. (2021). Digital transformation of global mobility markets. In *Mobility in Germany. Springer briefs in business*. Springer. https://doi.org/10.1007/978-3-030-71849-7_1

Gompers, P., Kaplan, S. N., & Mukharlyamov, V. (2016). What do private equity firms say they do? *Journal of Financial Economics, 121*(3), 449–476. https://doi.org/10.1016/j.jfineco.2016.06.003

Gompers, P. A., Gornall, W., Kaplan, S. N., & Strebulaev, I. A. (2020). How do venture capitalists make decisions? *Journal of Financial Economics, 135*(1), 169–190. https://doi.org/10.3386/w22587

Hamman, A., Nel, I., & Oberholzer, M. (2021). Analysing the criteria of private equity investment in South Africa. *Journal of Economic and Financial Sciences, 14*(1), 1–15. https://doi.org/10.4102/jef.v14i1.608

Hochberg, Y. V., Ljungqvist, A., & Lu, Y. (2007). Whom you know natters: Venture capital networks and investment performance. *The Journal of Finance, 62*(1), 251–301. https://doi.org/10.1111/j.1540-6261.2007.01207.x

Hsu, D. H. (2004). What do entrepreneurs pay for venture capital affiliation? *The Journal of Finance, 59*(4), 1805–1844. https://doi.org/10.1111/j.1540-6261.2004.00680.x

Lerner, J. (1994). The syndication of venture capital investments. *Financial Management, 23*(3), 16. https://doi.org/10.2307/3665618

Lerner, J., Schoar, A., & Wongsunwai, W. (2007). Smart institutions, foolish choices: The limited partner performance puzzle. *The Journal of Finance, 62*(2), 731–764. https://doi.org/10.1111/j.1540-6261.2007.01222.x

Lerner, J., Ledbetter, J., Speen, A., Leamon, A., & Allen, C. (2016). Private equity in emerging markets: Yesterday, today, and tomorrow. *The Journal of Private Equity, 19*(3), 8–20. https://doi.org/10.3905/jpe.2016.19.3.008

Megginson, W. L., & Weiss, K. A. (1991). Venture capitalist certification in initial public offerings. *The Journal of Finance, 46*(3), 879–903. https://doi.org/10.1111/j.1540-6261.1991.tb03770.x

Metzger, G. (2019). *KfW Start-up Monitor 2019. Start-up activity in Germany stabilizes: Intermediate stop or end of the downward slide? [KfW-Gründungsmonitor 2019. Gründungstätigkeit in Deutschland stabilisiert sich: Zwischenhalt oder Ende der Talfahrt?]*. KfW Bankengruppe. https://www.kfw.de/PDF/Download-Center/Konzernthemen/Research/PDF-Dokumente-Gründungsmonitor/KfW-Gruendungsmonitor-2019.pdf

Metzger, G. (2020a). *KfW start-up monitor 2020. Start-up activity in Germany in 2019: First increase in 5 years – 2020 in the shadow of the Corona pandemic [KfW-Gründungsmonitor 2020 Gründungstätigkeit in Deutschland 2019: erster Anstieg seit 5 Jahren – 2020 im Schatten der Corona- Pandemie]*. KfW Bankengruppe. https://www.kfw.de/PDF/Download-Center/Konzernthemen/Research/PDF-Dokumente-Gründungsmonitor/KfW-Gruendungsmonitor-2020.pdf

Metzger, G. (2020b). *KfW start-up report 2020. Start-ups in Germany stable at 70,000 in 2019 – Impact of Corona crisis uncertain [KfW-Start-up-Report 2020. Start-ups in Deutschland stabil bei 70.000 im Jahr 2019 – Auswirkung der Corona-Krise unsicher]*. KfW Bankengruppe. https://www.kfw.de/PDF/Download-Center/Konzernthemen/Research/KfW-Start-up-Report/KfW-Start-up-Report-2020.pdf

Metzger, G. (2020c). *KfW venture capital study 2020 VC market in Germany: Ripe for the next development step [KfW Venture Capital Studie 2020 VC-Markt in Deutschland: Reif für den nächsten Entwicklungsschritt]*. KfW Bankengruppe. https://www.kfw.de/PDF/Download-Center/Konzernthemen/Research/PDF-Dokumente-Studien-und-Materialien/KfW-Venture-Capital-Studie-2020.pdf

Muhammad, S., Li, Y., Wu, J., & Ali, G. (2017). Comparative analysis of venture capitalists investment criteria: A case from China and Pakistan. *Asia-Pacific Management Accounting Journal, 12*(2), 201–234.

Muzyka, D., Birley, S., & Leleux, B. (1996). Trade-offs in the investment decisons of European venture capitalists. *Journal of Business Venturing, 11*(4), 273–287. https://doi.org/10.1016/0883-9026(95)00126-3

Pozen, R. C. (2007). If private equity sized up your business. *Harvard Business Review, 85*(11), 78–87.

Puri, M., & Zarutskie, R. (2012). On the life cycle dynamics of venture-capital- and non-venture-capital-financed firms. *The Journal of Finance, 67*(6), 2247–2293. https://doi.org/10.1111/j.1540-6261.2012.01786.x

Schalast, C., & Wedell, G. (2019). Private equity [Private equity]. In C. Schalast & L. Raettig (Eds.), *Basics of the M&A business: Strategy – Law – Taxes [Grundlagen des M&A-Geschäftes: Strategie - Recht - Steuern]* (2nd ed., pp. 171–205). Springer.

Tyebjee, T. T., & Bruno, A. V. (1984). A model of venture capitalist investment activity. *Management Science, 30*(9), 1051–1066. https://doi.org/10.1287/mnsc.30.9.1051

Ueda, M. (2004). Banks versus venture capital: Project evaluation, screening, and expropriation. *The Journal of Finance, 59*(2), 601–621. https://doi.org/10.1111/j.1540-6261.2004.00643.x

Zacharakis, A. L., & Meyer, G. (1998). A lack of insight: Do venture capitalists really understand their own decision process? *Journal of Business Venturing, 13*(1), 57–76. https://doi.org/10.1016/s0883-9026(97)00004-9

Zopounidis, C. (1994). Venture capital modelling: Evaluation criteria for the appraisal of investments. *The Financier, 1*(2), 55–64.

Chapter 8
Research Design

8.1 Guided Expert Interview

The basic investment criteria used by private equity (PE) and venture capital (VC) investors when making investment decisions have already been addressed in several studies, but no significant literature has been identified that discusses specifically the investment criteria that venture capital investors apply when deciding whether to invest in a digital platform start-up in Germany. Considering the available literature, it is therefore not possible to identify clearly the criteria digital platform start-ups in Germany must meet in order to develop a strategy for generating equity through venture capital and, conversely, which investment criteria VC investors use when deciding whether to invest in digital platform start-ups in Germany.

During this study, a qualitative survey in the form of expert interviews was selected as the research method. A scientifically designed and detailed survey is an appropriate research method in this context because of its overarching goal of obtaining valid as well as authentic information about the respondents themselves, about additional stakeholders, about organizations involved in financing, or about specific topics by asking the respondents (Scholl, 2018).

Current research addresses the aspects but not process of transformation in innovation, management, and strategy (Friesendorf and Uedelhoven, 2021; Friesendorf and Uedelhoven, 2020). Due to this study's need for concrete examples from practice, expert interviews appeared to be a pragmatic method for gaining knowledge from experts who shared their practical experiences from various professional stations, resulting in qualitative, concrete implications for entrepreneurial practice and recommendations. While similar research results have already been published on general venture capital investment criteria, no identifiable research has been conducted on the specific topic of digital platform start-ups; in order to validate the hypotheses put forward by the experts, a deductive research approach was used to infer the general from the specific.

C. Friesendorf, N. J. Mir Haschemi, *Private Equity in Germany*, Business Guides on the Go, https://doi.org/10.1007/978-3-031-33708-6_8

As a result, the hypotheses established in this research approach are based on findings from related research on VC investment criteria. It is therefore the objective of the study to determine whether the already researched—but more general—investment criteria of VC investors are also relevant to their investment decisions regarding a digital platform start-up in Germany, and ultimately, to answer the overarching research question.

A guided interview process was used to conduct the expert interviews. A guided interview is defined by the survey instrument used to collect data for the guideline, while an expert interview is defined by the specific target group of the interviewees and the interest in expert knowledge as a distinct field of knowledge. Within the framework of the empirical study, the developed interview guideline provides a targeted framework and steering for expert interviews (Helfferich, 2014). In the following sections, we will describe how the expert interviews were evaluated and how the research questions were validated after the expert interviews.

8.2 Research Ethics

During conducting research, such as economic research, ethical concerns regarding societal principles and values may arise. A failure to address these ethical concerns will adversely affect the integrity of the research (Bryman & Bell, 2011). Even though business and management research rarely involve studies in which participants are adversely affected, ethical principles remain relevant.

This is an ethical issue that cannot be ignored. Therefore, a foundation of trust, as well as a precise declaration of consent, is essential in these research areas, while always protecting the interests of the respondents and safeguarding the integrity of the research (Easterby-Smith et al., 2015). To obtain the consent of voluntary participants, maintain protection and confidentiality, and ensure respect and ethical treatment, ethical principles and guidelines are followed in this research.

8.3 Research Questions and Hypotheses

Scientific hypotheses are value-free statements and assumptions about a predicted cause-and-effect relationship. Furthermore, they are considered essential for conceptualizing a research topic and are used to verify the consistency between theoretical and practical statements (Töpfer, 2012). Even though hypotheses generally express causal relationships, for example, in the form of "if-then statements," indicative "as-is statements" can also be utilized in substantive formulations.

The following are the eight hypotheses, as well as our research questions derived from the literature review. To establish, among other things, whether these criteria can be considered generally valid and can therefore also be applied as venture capital investment criteria in the context of German digital platform start-ups, these hypotheses are based on the existing literature on basic venture capital (VC) investment criteria.

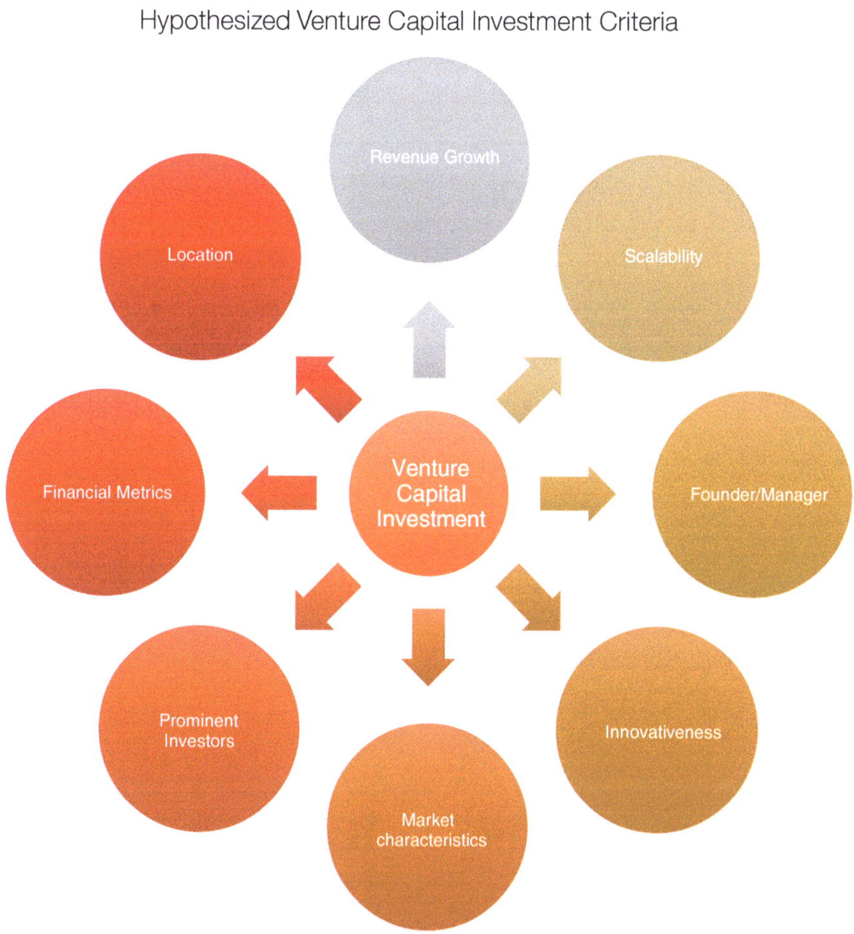

Fig. 8.1 Eight hypothesized venture capital criteria

Figures 8.1 and 8.2 illustrate the hypothesized criteria. As part of this study, the hypotheses presented will be empirically tested using the expert interviews, and the degree to which they can be confirmed will be examined.

8.4 Choice and Appraisal of Method

Interviews with experts were selected as the research method. An expert interview, as a structured variant of the guided interview, is a qualitative research method in which the interviewee is reduced in focus than the approach to exclusive bodies of knowledge (Liebold & Trinczek, 2009). The interview method aims to elicit perspectives and modes of action from experts. The objective of this research method is

List of Hypotheses to be tested using Guided Expert Interview Method

Criteria	No.	Hypothesis-Statement
Revenue growth	H1	Revenue growth is a VC investment criterion when deciding to invest in a digital platform start-up in Germany
Scalability	H2	Scalability is considered a VC investment criterion when deciding to invest in a digital platform start-up in Germany
Founder/Manager	H3	The founding/management team is considered a VC investment criterion when deciding to invest in a digital platform start-up in German
Innovativeness	H4	An innovative business idea is considered a VC investment criterion when deciding to invest in a digital platform start-up in Germany
Market characteristics	H5	Market characteristics are considered a VC investment criterion when deciding to invest in a digital platform start-up in Germany
Prominent Investors	H6	Well-known invested investors are considered a VC investment criterion when deciding to invest in a digital platform start-up in Germany
Financial Metrics	H7	Financial data is considered a VC investment criterion when deciding to invest in a digital platform start-up in Germany
Location	H8	Location is considered a VC investment criterion when deciding to invest in a digital platform start-up in Germany

Fig. 8.2 Eight list of hypotheses to be tested using guided interview method

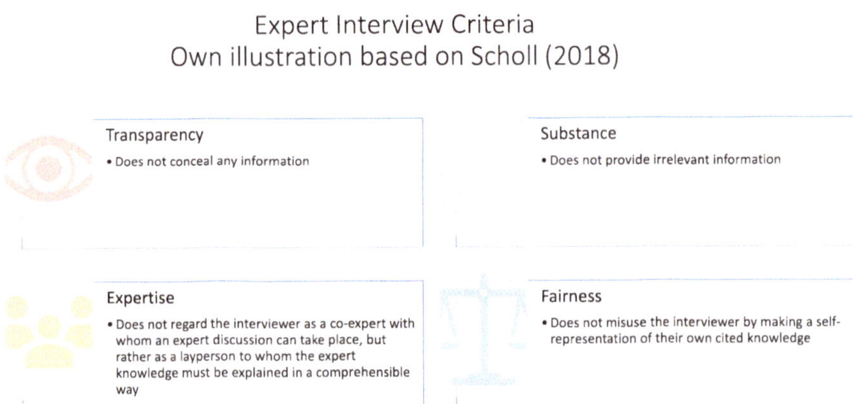

Fig. 8.3 Nine expert interview criteria

to have the expert confront the stated topic and problem and make profound statements because of this confrontation (Scholl, 2018).

For an expert interview to result in valid, useful information, the expert must be able to comment on the subject and the interview must be voluntary.

Figure 8.3 illustrates the requirements for an expert for this interview technique.

Interviews are conducted for the purpose of identifying what is common among the individual interviews, making statements about collectively shared knowledge, and generating area-specific and object-theoretical statements (Meuser & Nagel, 1991). The comparability of statements is best achieved by carefully selecting experts, considering the comparability of their positions, as well as their presumed comparable experience, and using a consistent interview guide.

According to Meuser and Nagel (1991), experts are responsible for designing, implementing, and controlling the solution to a problem or have access to information about certain groups of people or decision-making processes. The status of an expert therefore also results from the position or function that the expert holds within an organization, among other things, as well as the responsibility which the expert assumes for a specific task and the privileged access to the necessary information (Scholl, 2018). However, the assessment and identification of a person as an expert in the specific research process is always done by the researcher and, above all, must consider the context-specificity of the expert interviews in addition to who has privileged access to information and is accordingly willing to divulge it (Kaiser, 2014).

The research method chosen for this study is best suited because the research question is a subject-specific one that requires specialized knowledge and sufficient expertise to test the hypotheses and answer the overarching research question. Detailed information regarding the methodology and procedure of the survey can be found in the following sections.

8.5 Methodological Approach

In the following paragraphs, we provide insight into the methodological approach used for this empirical study. Further, we provide a description of how the study was conducted and how the results were derived. In addition to explaining the methodological procedure, the background of the survey is also presented in order to ensure reproducibility. Using a guideline-based questionnaire, expert interviews were conducted according to the research approach.

8.6 Selection of Experts

The overarching research question of this book was investigated using a qualitative research approach, with oral guided expert interviews conducted as an empirical method to investigate the research questions, i.e., to empirically test the hypotheses. Interviews of this type are a cost-effective option that, on the one hand, enable a transparent, detailed, and unique information content, and, on the other hand, allow reality to be revealed or brought to the attention of a wide public.

In turn, this leads to the extraction of concrete implications and recommendations for entrepreneurship practice. A qualitative research approach, on the other hand, requires only a relatively small number of participants who possess relevant specific knowledge, as opposed to quantitative research. The challenge with a qualitative method is finding potential experts who are willing to participate and who have the time and inclination to conduct an interview.

Our selection of experts was based on the following criteria as shown in the diagram 8.4 below. In addition to ensuring that appropriate experts were selected, these criteria ensured that they were sufficiently qualified as experts.

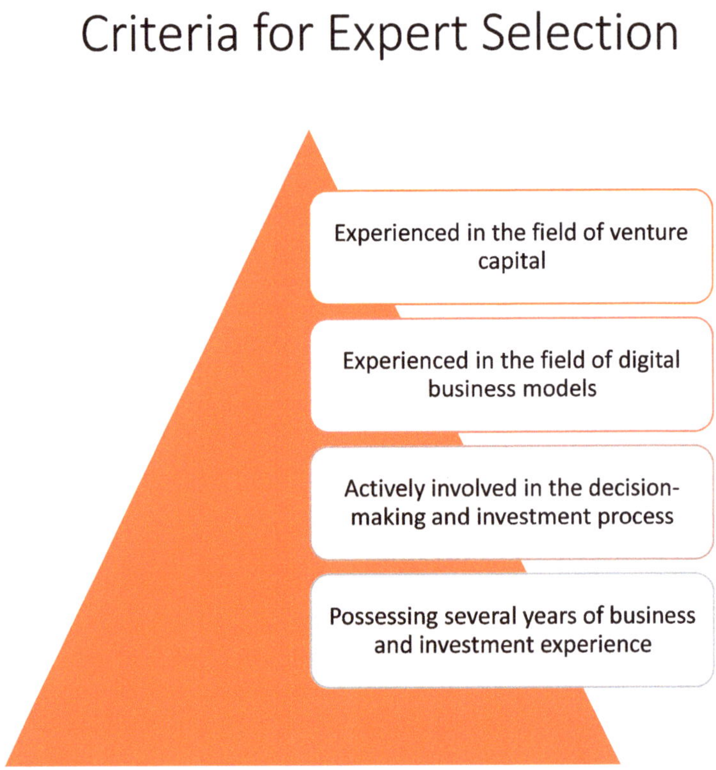

Fig. 8.4 Ten criteria for expert selection

Due to the relatively limited venture capital (VC) landscape in Germany, there are few opportunities to approach potential experts and conduct interviews. The research questions were thoroughly answered by contacting numerous experts based on their profiles, reputation, and expertise based on the criteria mentioned above and identified potential experts via professional networking platforms such as LinkedIn and Xing.

In this study, we conducted expert interviews with four individuals. While this number represents a rather small sample size, their exclusive, specific knowledge should nonetheless provide an approximately representative answer to the overarching research question. The experts were contacted via email, LinkedIn, and/or Xing and were informed about the authors, the motivation, the problem to be solved, the broader scope of the work, the hypotheses, and the interview structure.

Following the experts' agreement to participate in the survey, each received the consent form and the questionnaire on which the guided expert interview would be based. We ensured that the participants were able to view this questionnaire in advance of the interview in case they had any objections to answering any of the questions because their answers might contain sensitive information. Because the interviews were conducted during the COVID-19 pandemic, video teleconferencing software was used. A maximum of 45 min was allotted for each interview, which was recorded on a laptop and then transcribed. As a result of these transcripts, a qualitative analysis of the interviews was possible.

8.7 Interviewee Details

Here is a brief description of the four experts who have agreed to participate in this research. Anonymity was exercised by two of them.

INT Lars Kuppe has many years of experience in corporate finance, particularly in equity capital markets. He was involved in several IPOs and has served as a project manager for several capital market transactions. Additionally, he has assumed sector responsibility for digital business models within the ECM team. As Director of Private Markets (Private Equity & Venture Capital) at Bankhaus Lampe KG, he is responsible for both in-house private equity funds and the venture capital area.

The second expert (INT 1) holds a doctorate and works as an investment manager for a venture capital investor after holding various independent positions and C-level management positions. He is also a member of the board.

The third expert (INT 2), who is also a PhD, has held various positions in the investment sector, and is currently a partner at one of Europe's leading venture capital firms, responsible for managing German investment operations. Aside from holding several board positions, his main activities include managing the German portfolio and finding new investments in innovative and exciting start-ups.

INT Florian Weinkauf has extensive experience in the banking sector. In his role at Creditshelf AG, he is responsible for deal origination and market expansion for asset-light business models.

8.8 Guideline-Based Expert Interview

In this guideline, the expert interview will be structured and controlled in a targeted manner; it contains a list of all the relevant questions that should be asked during the interview and does not have a binding nature. Consequently, neither the order nor the specific formulation of the questions is predetermined. As a result of this relative openness, the interview can be tailored to the interviewee and follow-up questions can be asked if a topic has not been adequately addressed or if a topic has been raised by the interviewee (Hildebrandt, 2015).

Expert interviews were conducted in accordance with a guideline. In the context of conducting an expert interview, a well-prepared and structured guideline serves as a valuable control. To create a logically structured guideline, the interviewer must be familiar with the topic in advance. However, a variation of the guideline may also extend to the order of the questions: this may be adhered to or deviated from so that questions may be interspersed throughout the interview, depending on the situation.

It is also possible to vary the scope and degree of standardization of a guideline-based or expert interview. Among other things, the number of questions may vary, ranging from a few more general questions to many more detailed ones. The number of questions depends, however, on the length of the interview. A period of 1 h should only be exceeded in rare circumstances. It serves primarily as a memory aid for the interviewer rather than as a strict template for the interview.

Further, it helps structure the interview and enables comparison if the guideline contains many questions, and the sequence corresponds to a logic that is based on the content of the research question. Often, it is employed in the context of case studies with small samples in which the deeper perspective of the interviewees is pertinent. Open-ended questions are appropriate when interviewing experts, since limited answer options do not allow them to express their in-depth knowledge or adequately capture it (Scholl, 2018).

Here, experts are defined as advisors and knowledge brokers who have access to specific areas of knowledge and can impart factual and experiential knowledge. All interviews were conducted in accordance with the developed guidelines. Based on the similarity of the survey situation and the similarity of the questions asked, the individual interviews can easily be compared. To allow the broadest possible investigation of the research subject and the collection of information using paradigmatic questions, the questionnaire was oriented towards the course of the research work. During the development of the guideline, the questions were divided into seven topic blocks in accordance with the method recommended by Bogner et al. (2014).

In our interview guide, we begin with a brief introduction, in which we thank the experts for their participation and support, and then briefly describe the areas of thematic focus and the topic of this thesis. The guideline-supported expert interviews were conducted in German to ensure that the interview process could be as productive as possible, without losing any information due to language barriers.

Table 8.1 presents the list of our interview questions.

8.9 Data Preparation Based on Mayring's (2010) Content Analysis Method

A transcription of the expert interviews was conducted before they were evaluated according to Mayring's qualitative content analysis. Transcribing involves reproducing the experts' opinions, judgements, observations, and interpretations in the researcher's own words, according to Meuser and Nagel (1991). Although we transcribed the recordings word-for-word, the text was slightly altered linguistically. In general, introductory words, small talk, pause fillers, and word repetitions were eliminated.

Table 8.1 List of interview questions posed to our experts

Q1	How did you become interested in private equity (PE)/venture capital (VC)/start-ups/ digital platforms?
Q2	How long have you been involved with this topic and what is the reason for your interest in it?
Q3	What is your professional background?
Q4	What steps did you take to enter the company where you are currently working?
Q5	What is your specific area of responsibility?
Q6	How has the start-up environment, and especially the digital platform start-up environment, developed in Germany in recent years?
Q7	How has the general financing environment for start-ups, and especially for digital platform start-ups, developed in Germany in recent years?
Q8	How would you describe the development of the PE market, and especially, the VC market in Germany in recent years?
Q9	How would you describe the development of the VC environment in the context of financing start-ups, and in particular digital platform start-ups in Germany over the past few years? How would you evaluate the possibility of accessing this source of funding?
Q10	How do you see the importance and necessity of off-market equity financing, both PE and VC, for start-ups, and specifically for digital platform start-ups in Germany in the current climate?
Q11	How many potentially interesting and eligible digital platform start-ups do you analyze and evaluate within a year? In which phase is a contact established and what are the commonalities, differences, special features or even shortcomings of most of them?
Q12	What conditions must be in place for VC investors to show interest in financing a potential digital platform start-up?
Q13	What makes a digital platform start-up successful? What characteristics do you think most successful digital platform start-ups possess?
Q14	What role does the location or entrepreneurial ecosystem play in the general success of a digital platform start-up? What role does it play in terms of the funding environment?
Q15	How does this relate to the entrepreneurial ecosystem in Germany?
Q16	With regard to the statements, you made earlier, how do you see the future of VC as a form of equity financing in general, and in particular in the context of digital platform start-up financing in Germany? What challenges and opportunities do you see?
Q17	Is there anything else you would like to add to the interview?

As a result of the expert interviews, a large amount of information was analyzed qualitatively (specifically, text analysis); Mayring (2010) argues that this method of analysis is particularly appropriate for large amounts of data, for which it aims to provide an exact, systematic, and generalizing assessment. The purpose of this evaluation method is to arrange and structure information into a variety of forms, in this case interview transcripts, so that they can be analyzed and analyzed for scientific purposes. The use of this text-analytical method is comparatively the most common (Mayring & Fenzl, 2019).

Qualitative Content Analysis

Mayring (2010) describes three basic techniques of qualitative content analysis:

- To arrive at the core statements, summaries should reduce the text to its essential components. A prerequisite to this process is the formation of inductive categories.
- Explanations should be used to clarify unclear passages in the text.
- Cross-evaluations should be carried out by structuring the text material and highlighting certain aspects. To systematize the text, deductive categories are formed in advance.

With this method, one of the three techniques of text interpretation is used to describe and verify transcripts with content-analytical rules. There are two steps involved in applying these techniques. To begin, individual passages of content are assigned the theory-guided deductive categories. Next, it is necessary to determine whether a particular category may be assigned to more than one passage of text.

The creation of the category system is at the center of the procedure. The material is then processed according to this category system, and only the most relevant content passages that pertain to each category are considered. As a result, the analysis should be understandable. The goal of this method is to reduce the abundance of information and structure it towards the study's objective.

8.10 Limitations of Employed Research Method

It is imperative to point out the limitations of our research. Several limitations can be identified in the area of empirical research, particularly in relation to the processing and analysis of the data collected. Although the expert interviews were able to provide insights into practice, it remains unclear how far the expert statements may have deviated from the truth and to what extent such statements can provide an understanding of the real world.

Due to the voluntary nature of participation, some degree of transparency can be assumed as to the information and insight provided. Due to competition concerns, it is possible that additional internal investment criteria, information, and approaches have been withheld. Due to this, it is unclear whether the results and recommendations are considered by venture capital investors in their decision-making process.

Although four expert interviews were conducted, the small number of interviews could be considered a limitation within the context of the empirical study. Results are more likely to be applicable to a larger sample size. Furthermore, the empirical methodology may have been limited by an unintentional influence on the interview questions, thereby limiting the number of possible answers.

Furthermore, it is crucial to keep in mind that semantic falsification of statements within the context of the transcription of expert interviews is possible. This is due to linguistic or recording disturbances, and a potential loss of knowledge cannot be entirely ruled out. The wording of the questions may have also caused a distortion of expected answers, since too many aspects could have been considered in one question. The results of our interviews will be presented in the next chapter.

References

Bogner, A., Littig, B., & Menz, W. (2014). *Interviews with experts: A practice-oriented introduction [Interviews mit Experten: Eine praxisorientierte Einführung]*. Springer.

Bryman, A., & Bell, E. (2011). *Business research methods* (3rd ed.). Oxford University Press.

Easterby-Smith, M., Thorpe, R., & Jackson, P. R. (2015). *Management & business research* (5th ed.). SAGE.

Friesendorf, C., & Stern, J. (2020). Mangelnde Digitalisierung in der Finanzbranche. In *Digitalisierung des Auslandszahlungsverkehrs. essentials*. Springer. https://doi.org/10.1007/978-3-658-32738-5_1

Friesendorf, C., & Uedelhoven, L. (2021). Digital transformation of global mobility markets. In *Mobility in Germany. Springer briefs in business*. Springer. https://doi.org/10.1007/978-3-030-71849-7_1

Helfferich, C. (2014). Guided and expert interviews [Leitfaden- und Experteninterviews]. In N. Baur & J. Blasius (Eds.), *Handbook of methods of empirical social research [Handbuch Methoden der empirischen Sozialforschung]* (pp. 559–574). Springer.

Hildebrandt, A. (2015). Expert interviews [Experteninterview]. In A. Hildebrandt, S. Jäckle, F. Wolf, & A. Heindl (Eds.), *Methodology, methods, research design: A textbook for advanced students of political science [Methodologie, Methoden, Forschungsdesign: Ein Lehrbuch fur fortgeschrittene Studierende der Politikwissenschaft]* (pp. 241–256). Springer.

Kaiser, R. (2014). Planning and conducting qualitative expert interviews [Die Planung und Durchführung qualitativer Experteninterviews]. In H. G. Ehrhart, B. Frevel, K. Schubert, & S. S. Schüttemeyer (Eds.), *Conceptual and methodological foundations of qualitative expert interviews [Konzeptionelle und methodologische Grundlagen qualitativer Experteninterviews]* (pp. 21–50). Springer.

Liebold, R., & Trinczek, R. (2009). Expert interviews [Experteninterviews]. In S. Kühl, P. Strodtholz, & A. Taffertshofer (Eds.), *Handbook methods of organisational research: Quantitative and qualitative methods [Handbuch Methoden der Organisationsforschung: Quantitative und Qualitative Methoden]* (pp. 32–56). Springer.

Mayring, P. (2010). Qualitative content analysis [Qualitative Inhaltsanalyse]. In G. Mey & K. Mruck (Eds.), *Handbook qualitative research in psychology [Handbuch qualitative Forschung in der Psychologie]* (pp. 601–613). Springer.

Mayring, P., & Fenzl, T. (2019). Qualitative content analysis [Qualitative Inhaltsanalyse]. In N. Baur & J. Blasius (Eds.), *Handbook methods of empirical social research [Handbuch Methoden der empirischen Sozialforschung]* (2nd ed., pp. 633–648). Springer.

Meuser, M., & Nagel, U. (1991). *Expert interviews – Much tried, little thought: a contribution to the qualitative methodological discussion [ExpertInneninterviews - vielfach erprobt, wenig bedacht: ein Beitrag zur qualitativen Methodendiskussion]*. In D. Garz & K. Kraimer (Eds.), *Qualitative-empirical social research: concepts, methods, analyses [Qualitativ-empirische Sozialforschung: Konzepte, Methoden, Analysen]* (pp. 441–471). Westdt. Verlag. https://nbn-resolving.org/urn:nbn:de:0168-ssoar-24025

Scholl, A. (2018). *The interview [Die Befragung]* (4th ed.). UVK.

Töpfer, A. (2012). Chapter F. How are cause-effect relationships/hypotheses to be elaborated as core pieces of epistemological research? – Hypothesis forms/types and hypothesis generation - [Kapitel F. Wie sind Ursachen-Wirkungs-Zusammenhänge/ Hypothesen als Kern- stücke erkenntniswissenschaftlicher Forschungen herauszuarbeiten? – Hypothesenformen/ -arten und Hypothesenbildung –]. In A. Töpfer (Ed.), *Successful research: A guide for bachelor's, master's and doctoral students [Erfolgreich Forschen: Ein Leitfaden für Bachelor-, Master-Studierende und Doktoranden]* (3rd ed., pp. 176–216). Springer.

Chapter 9
Research Analyses and Results

9.1 Founding and/or Managing Team

Our interviews and evaluations of the digital platform start-ups indicate that one of the most important criteria that determines whether a digital platform start-up is eligible for private equity (PE) or venture capital (VC) financing can be the founder and/or her management team. Below are quotes from the interview transcripts that support our hypothesis.

9.1.1 Diversity of Team Skills, Tech-World Knowhow and Marketing

The team is ultimately one of the most important factors in making a decision about investing in a digital platform start-up, according to INT Kuppe. According to INT Kuppe, it is important for the team to have individuals with different skills but also for the team to harmonize (cf. INT Kuppe, 00:24:52, lines 293–302): "That is what I always hear from the conversations, that in the end it's also a lot about the team. In a team like this, you always have to cover different skills. There has to be someone who knows the tech world well, and who can, so to speak, cover all the processes digitally relatively quickly. Afterward, you have to have someone who knows the marketing area well, so that you can make the platform known as quickly as possible. You have to have salespeople who can get suppliers and customers onto this platform. So then, on the one hand you need a well-harmonized team and on the other hand, you also need different skills within the team." (cf. INT Kuppe, 00: 24:52, lines 293–302)

C. Friesendorf, N. J. Mir Haschemi, *Private Equity in Germany*, Business Guides on the Go, https://doi.org/10.1007/978-3-031-33708-6_9

9.1.2 Conviction of Idea and Founder/Team Drive

INT 1 (00:18:49, lines 265–268) also confirms the importance of the team: "So, I think one of the most important points is and remains the team. [...] At the end of the day, I think it is really just the two points of idea and team." (cf. INT 1, 00:18:49, lines 265–268). In particular, according to INT 1 (00:19:05, line 272–282), it is crucial that the team is trusted to follow through with the idea and build it up successfully, even if difficulties should arise: "And that is simply because, especially with the team, there is a certain drive towards the goal. So it is simple, you seem to notice relatively quickly whether someone has the drive, it can be someone who either already has a lot of experience [...] It can also be someone who simply has the drive, who you trust to really pull it off and build it to success and then also grit their teeth when things get difficult. [...] There are always difficult phases and if you do not have the bite, it will be difficult. In any case, it is a point on which we place a strong focus. The team." (cf. INT 1, 00:19:05, lines 272–282)

9.1.3 Sales Force and Process-Orientation

Additionally, INT 2 (00:18:56, lines 282–287) indicates that investors prefer organizations in which the sales department has already hired people and has made basic progress in this area. The lack of sufficient human sales capabilities and competencies is therefore considered to be one of the primary reasons for rejection. INT 2 indicates that in such a case, the VC investors would first need to develop a proper sales team within the context of a completed investment, without knowing in advance whether the sales approach would be successful. Accordingly, the sales experience of the team is also an important factor in the selection of investment opportunities (cf. INT 2, 00:18:56, lines 282–287): "And of course, we like to have organizations that have already set up proper processes in their sales and we invest in them. But we also often see that they still have one or two salespeople and maybe even the CEO still does it himself. That when we come in, we first have to set it up properly. That is always one of the core reasons for rejection [...] We cannot yet say whether your sales will work at all. I think that is an important point in the selection here." (cf. INT 2, 00:18:56, lines 282–287)

9.1.4 Multiple Founders, Clarity of Goal, and Ambition

INT 2 (00:18:56, lines 288–291) further states that as a VC investor, they also like to see more than one founder in the team: "To be honest, we always like to have more than one founder, simply because there is a bit more redundancy and they complement each other more." (cf. INT 2, 00:18:56, lines 288–291)

INT 2 (00:24:57, lines 310–313) also confirms that VC investors who invest primarily in earlier stages consider the (start-up) team to be the most important aspect. Knowledge about their expertise and what goals they are pursuing is therefore particularly relevant. In addition, they must be seen as ambitious vis-à-vis the VC investor: "That may be a little different for earlier investing VCs, and I will separate that very briefly, at enjoying ventures the most important thing for us was that we get to know the founding team, that we know a little bit about their expertise, where they want to go, and they have to be ambitious for us [...]." (cf. INT 2, 00: 24:57, lines 310–313)

9.1.5 *Pitching Quality and Argumentative Efficiency as Vital to Seed Investors*

According to INT 2 (00:24:57, lines 319–321), seed investors in particular strongly focus on the team: "And I think it is typical for seed investors like us at the time that we have a stronger focus on the team [...]." (cf. INT 2, 00:24:57, lines 319–321). However, beyond seed investors specifically, according to INT 2 (00:24:57, lines 326–330), the team continues to be extremely important for VC investors investing in later stages: "And that is where the focus goes a little bit, so founders are still extremely important and we see that the teams there also have to have significantly more quality than in the seed area because they have often been supplemented or have simply learned." (cf. INT 2, 00:24:57, lines 326–330)

Essentially, as INT 2 (00:27:47, lines 344–346) states later in the interview, a VC investor can go into great detail regarding the aspects to be considered, but ultimately the team will again turn out to be of utmost importance: "Yes, exactly, that is it so roughly. I mean, you can go into as much detail as you like, of course, about everything we pay attention to. But I think the team is the most important thing." (cf. INT 2, 00:27:47, lines 344–346)

INT Weinkauf also confirmed that the quality of the founding management team is used as a criterion when deciding whether to invest in a digital platform start-up in Germany (cf. INT Weinkauf, 00:14:06, lines 192–196): "I think if you have something good to get seed funding together, you have a good pitch, you have good planning to really get investors together, if you have a reasonably good topic and you do not have two complete idiots sitting together now, I think that it is a relatively good time." (cf. INT Weinkauf, 00:14:06, lines 192–196)

9.1.6 *Conclusion*

Taking into account the statements made by all four experts, the practical findings confirm that VC investors use the founding/management team as a criterion for investing in German digital platform companies. The statements indicate that a good team is a prerequisite for a digital platform start-up to obtain equity financing through VC in Germany.

9.2 Innovativeness

In the previous chapters, we have pointed out that innovativeness is identified in research as one of the most important factors for the survival of a start-up and as a criterion for attracting PE via VC into the company (Friesendorf and Uedelhoven, 2021; Friesendorf and Stern, 2020). To substantiate this claim, we have presented below the opinions of the experts in order to do so. It is our definition that innovativeness can be defined as being the content of a business idea that has clearly identified innovations aspects such that the business idea is radically new in the marketplace.

9.2.1 Uniqueness and Market Differentiation

INT Kuppe (00:14:28, lines 169–171) points out that gaining access to capital from investors is not an easy task, especially if investors are not aware of the specific features and characteristics that set this particular digital platform apart from others. The targeted market that is appropriate for the establishment of a digital platform is one that is particularly relevant to the establishment of a digital platform.: "Not easily. You have to make it clear what you want to do, how you stand out from other digital platforms, or why this market, in particular, is predestined for founding a digital platform." (cf. INT Kuppe, 00:14:28, lines 169–171)

INT 1 (00:12:07, lines 174–175 & 182–185) also argues that although the funding environment has developed positively, VC funding is still not easy, and therefore having a good business model idea is a fundamental prerequisite for the realization of financing. Although according to INT 1, evaluating whether an idea is a good one is difficult, objective evaluation standards can be applied at some points in the evaluation process: "It has certainly developed positively, but still, [...] getting VC funding is still nothing easy. [...] Of course, it always presupposes that you have a good idea. Now, of course, it is always difficult to judge whether the idea is good or not. At one point or another, you can perhaps apply a certain degree of objectivity and say, okay, that's definitely something that's not completely wrong." (cf. INT 1, 00:12:07, lines 174–175 & 182–185)

9.2.2 Functionality of Business Idea

Fundamentally, INT 1 (00:18:49, lines 266–267) argues that the existence of a good idea should be seen as an essential prerequisite, because if VC investors did not believe in the idea, then no funding would be forthcoming: "So sure, you need a good idea, of course. [...] if we do not believe in the idea, then the topic is done for us. That is clear." (cf. INT 1, 00:18:49, lines 266–267).

INT 2 (00:18:56, lines 267–268) also confirms that a potential flaw in the business model, and thus a potentially flawed idea, is seen by VC investors as an exclusion criterion in an investment decision: "So, you have to distinguish between, they have some lack in the business model that we don't think is good [...]." (cf. INT 2, 00:18:56, lines 267–268)

INT Weinkauf further confirms that with a good business model, capital will always be realized (cf. INT Weinkauf, 00:14:06, lines 190–192): "[...] the market is so brutally big, you will always get money if you have a good business model." (cf. INT Weinkauf, 00:14:06, lines 190–192)

9.2.3 Business Model as a Solution

A further argument made by INT Weinkauf (00:23:23, lines 300–302) is that the importance of placing a clear emphasis on the unique selling proposition (USP) as well as the basic fact that a digital platform start-up would actually be able to solve a problem that others cannot. From the investor's point of view, these factors were particularly critical to raising capital.: "Yes, where is your USP? What do you do better than someone else at the end of the day? What problem do you solve? The classic VC questions. Just see the case, understand the case." (cf. INT Weinkauf, 00: 23:23, lines 300–302). INT Weinkauf (00:23:23, lines 309–311) repeatedly emphasizes the importance of this question: "But where is the USP, I cannot tell you how often I have heard this question or asked it myself. But that is really the question, yes, what do you do better than the others?" (cf. INT Weinkauf, 00:23:23, lines 309–311)

9.2.4 Patents and Buyer Power

Although it is uncommon for digital platform start-ups to file and obtain patents at the early stage, our interviews showed that VC investors are definitely interested in start-ups that do have the potential of gaining patents so as to secure market space and/or leadership (cf. INT Weinkauf, 00:23:23, lines 306–309): "There are usually no patents for a platform start-up, because they don't really have their own product, but this may arise. But VC investors actually find that quite exciting." (cf. INT Weinkauf, 00:23:23, lines 306–309). However, according to INT Weinkauf (00:

25:37, lines 342–344), investors essentially focus on whether the information available to them explains that the digital platform start-up solves a problem and will attract customers (cf. INT Weinkauf, 00:25:37, lines 342–344): "[...] can you read somewhere that this problem they are supposedly solving is also being solved? Is there a buyer for it?" (cf. INT Weinkauf, 00:25:37, lines 342–344)

9.2.5 Conclusion

It is evident that all the experts who made statements cited the importance of a good business model or a good idea in their statements. The practical findings from these statements confirm that VC investors in Germany use the existence of a unique idea as one of the criteria when deciding whether to invest in a digital platform start-up that is operating in the digital space. As a result, it can be conclusively stated that the existence of an innovative business idea is a criterion that a digital platform start-up must fulfill in order to secure equity financing through VC in Germany in order to realize their dream of becoming a successful company.

9.3 Market Attractiveness

As a result of our research, it was concluded that the value of the market and its attractiveness to be involved as a stakeholder could be a critical factor for private equity (PE) and venture capital (VC) investments to be successful (Friesendorf and Uedelhoven, 2021). This hypothesis is substantiated by the analysis below based on the content of the interviews.

9.3.1 Value of the Online Market

According to INT Kuppe (00:23:28, lines 278–284), when considering the characteristics of the market, it is particularly important to make investors understand why there is a need to replace the offline market. In addition, it is particularly relevant to closely examine the competitors: "[...] and also accordingly, when I think of a digital platform, there is often also an offline market. First of all, there has to be a necessity to replace offline trade, so to speak. And then it is often the case that you have to look very closely at the competition. Are there perhaps already platforms that operate digitally, that perhaps operate in neighboring markets and can very easily cover their own niche in the future?" (cf. INT Kuppe, 00:23:28, lines 278–284).

9.3.2 Size of the Identified Market

INT 1 (00:19:05, lines 282–284) also confirms the relevance of market characteristics, which should be taken into account above all when assessing the persuasiveness of an idea. According to INT 1 (00:19:05, lines 282–284), the market characteristics and the conviction of an idea are interconnected; it is therefore particularly important that the market is large enough: "And sure, we have to be convinced of the idea per se as well, of course. And that is also connected to the market to a certain extent, of course. So, the market is big enough." (cf. INT 1, 00:19:05, lines 282–284)

INT 2 (00:18:56, lines 271–271) also confirms that the size of the market is of particular relevance from the perspective of VC investors: "[...] or the market must be big enough." (cf. INT 2, 00:18:56, lines 271–271)

9.3.3 Minimum Viable Product and Uncontested Markets

Furthermore, INT 2 (00:24:57, lines 314–319) states that, in an interesting and growing market, a start-up should show that it has a product, either a Minimum Viable Product (MVP) or a final product, which will show the VC investors that the product works in the market. In addition, new areas should be digitized. Accordingly, the consideration of competition is relevant: "[...] theoretically, which is in a market that is interesting and growing and that they are able to comprehensibly show that they can come up with a product, or that they usually already have an MVP or a finished product for which we can see that it works and that they are digitizing an area that has not yet been so strongly contested. So, competition is of course also a factor here [...]." (cf. INT 2, 00:24:57, lines 314–319)

Furthermore, INT 2 (00:18:56, lines 267–270) confirms that features such as a potential shortage in the market will also lead to sorting out and thus choosing other start-ups: "So, you have to distinguish between, they have some lack [...] that we do not think is good or in the market, for example, [...] which is why we sort them out against other start-ups that we think are better." (cf. INT 2, 00:18:56, lines 267–270)

9.3.4 Potential Market Monopoly and Niche-Building

INT Weinkauf additionally states that the market and its associated characteristics are also used as criteria for an investment decision. It should be clear to investors where exactly the potential market is located and, if applicable, which specific niche the digital platform start-up has discovered for itself. According to INT Weinkauf, it is therefore necessary for digital platform start-ups to develop a niche and take a monopoly position there (cf. INT Weinkauf, 00:23:23, lines 302–304): "Where is the market? [...] Where is the niche, if any, that you have discovered for yourself?

[...] Always go into the niche and build a monopoly eventually [...]." (cf. INT Weinkauf, 00:23:23, lines 302–304)

9.3.5 *Conclusion*

In their statements, all the experts cited market characteristics as criteria for potentially interesting financing. Based on the practical findings from these statements, it can be confirmed that the market characteristics are potential criteria that VC investors use when deciding whether to invest in a digital platform start-up in Germany. According to the statements, it can therefore be confirmed that the characteristics of the market represent criteria that a digital platform start-up must consider in order to realize off-market equity financing by VC in Germany.

9.4 Financial Metrics

We identified financial figures, data, and metrics to be an important factor for private equity (PE) and venture capital (VC) as detailed in literature on innovation and financial strategy (Friesendorf and Stern, 2020). We present below our findings.

9.4.1 *Business Plan as Nice-to-Have*

With regard to financial figures, INT 2 (00:24:57, lines 320–324) states that a business plan is basically worthless in the initial phases, especially in the seed phase, as it is almost impossible to derive meaningful figures or values from it in terms of financial data. However, from a VC point of view, the business plan can provide an insight into the founders' thinking, the scaling potential, and forecasts of potential costs, and could thus be compared with their own assessments: "And I think it is typical for seed investors like us at the time [...] and of course cannot deduce much from the numbers yet. [...] Business plans in the seed sector are worth almost nothing, to be honest. We use it to somehow find out how the founders think, how it could scale, what are appropriate (unv.) costs they calculate with and does our opinion match with that." (cf. INT 2, 00:24.57, lines 320–324). INT Weinkauf argues that ultimately, for investors, understanding the business case can be seen as a basic prerequisite (cf. INT Weinkauf, 00:23:23, lines 320–321): "[...] but also, we just want to understand the business case." (cf. INT Weinkauf, 00:23:23, lines 320–321)

9.4.2 Customer Acquisition as Key Metric

Furthermore, according to INT Weinkauf, the performance of the units of economics and thus the key performance indicators (KPIs) is also decisive. Such information is crucial, as this ultimately allows conclusions to be drawn about whether the digital platform start-up had a functioning product or business model (cf. INT Weinkauf, 00:25:37, lines 332–339): "[...] how do your units of economics perform, i.e. where do you have customer growth or do you have a huge churn where all the customers jump away again after 3 months and that speaks for a non-functioning product. That is the way we think about it in the end. And then you just want to see (unv.) the number of customers grows, how long they stay, how often they sell, they buy, depending on what kind of business model it is. Typically retention, churn, where you simply go down to the KPIs [...]." (cf. INT Weinkauf, 00:25:37, lines 332–339)

9.4.3 Customer Retention Rate and Key Account Management

According to INT Weinkauf, the units of economics are crucial, especially the retention rate, because since the acquisition costs for customers are relatively expensive, the platform should keep each individual customer for as long as possible (cf. INT Weinkauf, 00:28:05, lines 363–370): "So, in the end, it is the unit economics in different forms or with different weighting, but it is actually always the unit economics that is decisive. And of course, the most important thing is always retention, i.e., how long do I keep the customer? Because in most cases, regardless of whether it is finance, e-commerce, software or anything else in that direction, I always spend a relatively large amount of money on my acquisition costs, and I want to keep the key account for as long as possible, in principle over the lifetime value of the key account, which then means retention." (cf. INT Weinkauf, 00:28:05, lines 363–370)

9.4.4 Conclusion

In their statements, only two experts cited financial data as a potential criterion for financing that would be interesting. According to these statements, one can conclude that while financial data can be regarded as a criterion in order to decide whether to invest in a digital platform start-up in Germany, it is not a criterion that is used by all VC investors, as opposed to the criteria we discussed previously. There can be no doubt that financial data can be considered a criterion based on these findings, but it should be noted that it was not as heavily weighted as the criteria that had previously been considered.

9.5 Scalability

Due to the fact that exponential growth has been touted as an important aspect of the start-up world, we hypothesized that scalability of the start-up business model might be a criterion for private equity (PE) via venture capital (VC) investment. Below are the arguments presented by our experts.

9.5.1 *Scalability Enhances Valuation*

INT Kuppe (00:02:36, lines 30–36) emphasizes that as soon as a platform is successfully established which enables access to numerous users, it is possible to scale the business model quite quickly. Conversely, this would also make it possible to arouse the interest of investors, and ultimately, high scalability would also lead to high company valuations, as the VC industry is less concerned with profitability than with growth opportunities: "This means that once you have successfully established a platform on which many customers gather together, or [...] where you have access to good customers, it is possible to scale your business model relatively quickly. And accordingly, this is also very interesting for investors. And that results in principle in high company valuations; perhaps more than in any other industry, profitability plays only a subordinate role in this segment. The main thing here is growth." (cf. INT Kuppe, 00:02:36, lines 30–36)

9.5.2 *Pace of Critical Mass*

In addition, INT Kuppe (00:05:42, lines 86–90) emphasizes that a necessary condition for scaling up quickly is to rapidly reach critical mass, making it more difficult for competitors to access the market: "And I believe that once you have a player who has established such a platform that has reached critical mass, it is very difficult for other companies to gain a foothold there and therefore I believe that there are still niches where you can also develop digital platforms, but you just have to be fast and you have to scale extremely quickly." (cf. INT Kuppe, 00:05:42, lines 86–90).

9.5.3 *Exponential User Growth*

INT Kuppe (00:15:15, lines 179–184) cites fast scalability as the main factor in building a digital platform, as it is especially important to be fast at the beginning, since a platform only becomes interesting when it attracts as many users as possible: "It is all about scalability. Especially at the beginning, it is important to be very fast and you always have this chicken-and-egg problem. You only become interesting when as many people as possible are on the platform and for the end customers this platform is only interesting when there is also a correspondingly large offer, in other words, you always have to deal with both sides [...].” (cf. INT Kuppe, 00:15:15, lines 179–184)

Furthermore, INT Kuppe (00:23:28, lines 277–278) attributes the need for rapid scalability to the fact that it demonstrates to VC investors that a digital platform can grow rapidly in a market: “Yes, so on the one hand there has to be scalability, so that you can see that it is possible to grow in the market within a very short time [...].” (cf. INT Kuppe, 00:23:28, lines 277–278)

9.5.4 Scalability as Founders' Attribute

INT 2 (00:24:57, lines 324–326) also emphasizes that VC investors validate the business model when assessing whether an investment should be made, but this is primarily to assess the founding team and whether the VC investor sees scaling potential: “So it is more of a validation of the business model, whether they have fundamentally understood what they are doing, whether we see enough scaling potential there.” (cf. INT 2, 00:24:57, lines 324–326)

INT 2 (00:27:47, lines 346–347) also confirms that the growth and potential growth of a digital platform start-up is particularly important for VC investors: “Growth, growth is of course also very important.” (cf. INT 2, 00:27:47, lines 346–347). INT Weinkauf also confirms that it is important for investors to know where the growth will be (cf. INT Weinkauf, 00:23:23, lines 302–302).

9.5.5 Conclusion

A criterion for potentially interesting funding cited by all but one of the experts is scalability. As a result of these practical findings, we are able to confirm that VC investors use scalability as a criterion for determining whether to invest in a digital platform start-up in Germany. Based on the statements, it can be concluded that scalability is a criterion a digital platform start-up must meet in order to obtain equity financing through VC in Germany (INT 1, 2021; INT 2, 2021; INT Kuppe, 2021; INT Weinkauf, 2021).

9.6 Prominent Investor

The results of our study suggest that well-known or prominent investors may increase the chances of getting funded through private equity (PE) and venture capital (VC). During our interview process, we were able to find out the following information.

9.6.1 Investors as Endorsers

Regarding already existing well-known investors, INT Kuppe (00:16:26, lines 198–203) argues that it will improve a start-up's reputation if a VC investor who is established in the market is already invested. Moreover, their investment in a digital platform start-up could be understood as a kind of endorsement, which will thus facilitate the acquisition of customers as well as strategically useful stakeholders: "On the other hand, these VCs often already have experience in the area of digital platforms and can help strategically, and it always serves to improve the reputation if an established VC player invests in a start-up, which is also a bit of a distinction for a start-up and makes it easier to get customers and strategic people for this platform." (cf. INT Kuppe, 00:16:26, lines 198–203).

9.6.2 Tier-1 Investors Enhance Start-up Competitiveness

INT Weinkauf confirmed this, saying that winning a good Tier-1 investor would certainly be considered a competitive advantage for a digital platform start-up (cf. INT Weinkauf, 00:16:29, lines 233–235): "I would actually say, to answer the question clearly, yes, if you have a VC investor in there, a good Tier 1 VC investor, that is definitely a competitive advantage." (cf. INT Weinkauf, 00:16:29, lines 233–235)

9.6.3 Conclusion

Two experts were the only ones to cite the presence of well-known or prominent investors as one of the most important criterion for assessing a company within the scope of the evaluation. In conclusion, it can be proved that the presence of an already invested investor can be considered as a criterion, but it is not a criterion that is used by all venture capital investors in Germany when they are deciding whether to invest in a digital platform start-up in Germany. In conclusion, it can be stated that the presence of an investor who is already invested can be considered to be a criterion, but that it is not as heavily weighed as some other criteria may be.

9.7 Revenue Growth

The aspect of specific revenue growth was not explicitly mentioned by any expert in the context of the evaluation, and therefore, it can be concluded that venture capital (VC) investors do not use revenue growth as a criterion when deciding about investing in a digital platform startup in Germany. Accordingly, the survey did not confirm that potential revenue growth is a criterion that digital platform start-ups must meet in order to obtain off-market equity financing from VCs in Germany.

9.8 Location

INT 1 (00:23:51, lines 341–344) argues that location is irrelevant in the context of the financing environment and thus in terms of influencing an investment decision: "But that's why I think it's quite irrelevant in many places. In terms of financing, because relatively few people invest money in it, and also in terms of the environment as a whole." (cf. INT 1, 00:23:51, lines 341–344)

The influence of a location on an investment decision by venture capital (VC) investors was only mentioned by one expert during the evaluation. On the basis of this, it can be concluded that location is not used as a criterion by VC investors when making a decision about investing in a digital platform start-up in Germany. Accordingly, the survey did not confirm that the influence of location is a criterion that digital platform start-ups must take into account in order to realize equity financing through VC in Germany.

References

Friesendorf, C., & Stern, J. (2020). Mangelnde Digitalisierung in der Finanzbranche. In *Digitalisierung des Auslandszahlungsverkehrs. essentials*. Springer. https://doi.org/10.1007/978-3-658-32738-5_1

Friesendorf, C., & Uedelhoven, L. (2021). Digital transformation of global mobility markets. In *Mobility in Germany. Springer briefs in business*. Springer. https://doi.org/10.1007/978-3-030-71849-7_1

INT 1. (2021, August 13). *Transcript of the expert interview*.

INT 2. (2021, August 27). *Transcript of the expert interview*.

INT Kuppe, L. (2021, August 10). *Transcript of the expert interview*.

INT Weinkauf, F. (2021, August 31). *Transcript of the expert interview*.

Chapter 10
Summary and Recommendations

10.1 Research Design Summary

We have attempted to unravel the financial and funding aspects of start-ups in Germany in this book in order to provide a basis for future research. Taking into account the growing availability of technological options in the American, European, and Asian continents, it is evident that there is a great deal of interest in the start-up world when it comes to understanding the conditions necessary and sufficient to obtain financial resources that are necessary to fuel and sustain the growth of start-up businesses. The fact that Germany has multiple advantages in terms of its geographical location in Europe, a high per capita income that allows for a start-up culture, and a high level of venturesome stakeholders make it an ideal candidate for our research.

In order to understand the German market, we asked ourselves the following question: Which criteria must be met by a digital platform start-up in order to obtain equity financing through venture capital in Germany? To achieve this objective, we began by researching and presenting the relevant theoretical foundations that are crucial to gaining a deeper understanding of the young and not yet established topic of start-ups in management sciences, as well as attempting to place this topic in the same context as other objects of study in management sciences. It was a great pleasure to discuss the concept, idea, and motivation behind start-ups, the aspects involved in making a start-up successful on the highly competitive market, and the stages involved in the financing or funding of start-ups at all stages.

As a result of our research, we were able to identify eight factors that could be used by a venture capitalist to form a basis or influence his or her decision when he or she is scouring the market for promising start-up companies in order to invest in. Our primary goal in this study was to answer our broader research questions by identifying these factors as hypotheses. Aiming to fill a gap in the literature on start-up financing, especially in the context of digital platform startups, and furthermore in the context of an unexplored start-up market in Germany, our goal is to contribute to

C. Friesendorf, N. J. Mir Haschemi, *Private Equity in Germany*, Business Guides on the Go, https://doi.org/10.1007/978-3-031-33708-6_10

the scarce literature on start-up financing. It is our firm belief that filling this gap will enable all stakeholders in the German start-up ecosystem to collaborate and encourage more participants to venture into the market, and through our research, founders, managers, and financiers will be able to better prepare for the market, in other words, they will be able to design strategies to obtain venture capital in a more effective manner. The reason for this is as well that we are convinced that start-ups will become one of the most critical components of the overall economic setup in the country in the years to come.

We adopted qualitative methods of survey design and interviewing in order to test and validate our eight hypotheses. Using a sample of four interviewees who are experts in Germany on start-ups, digital platform start-ups, and financing start-ups, we conducted an empirical study and generated primary data by interviewing them.

In order to obtain as much information about: private equity, venture capital financing methods, start-up prospects, stakeholder motivation and behavior, digital platform industry constructs and perceptions of success as possible, we formulated questions to obtain as much information as possible.

The data collection was done through qualitative expert interviews of decision-makers who had been involved in detail in the investment selection process over a period of time. We tested our eight hypotheses based on a qualitative content analysis of the data collected in this study. As part of this study, we aimed to determine whether the investment criteria already cited in the literature are also used by VC investors when deciding whether or not to invest in a digital platform start-up in Germany. Conversely, establishing this should simultaneously answer the research question that is being asked. In order to find out whether the findings from the literature research could be validated from the expert interviews and the analysis of the derived data, we conducted expert interviews and analyzed the derived data. As a result, the findings of the literature were to be validated by means of confirmation and compared as to the degree of confirmation of the findings. By using a guidelines-based interview method, the data were intended to be analyzed and compared in an objective manner to achieve target-oriented evaluation and comparability. We presented the results in the previous chapter.

10.2 Discussion of Results

According to the empirical study, most of the criteria derived from the existing literature are also applied when a venture capital (VC) investor decides to invest in a start-up digital platform in Germany according to the criteria derived from the literature. When it comes to investing in a digital platform start-up in Germany, investors use the same investment criteria in most cases, although their explanations vary.

10.2.1 Primary Criteria

The evaluation indicated that the criteria of founding/management team (Q3), innovativeness, i.e., an innovative business idea (Q4) and market characteristics (Q5) are particularly relevant, having been unanimously cited and thus confirmed by the experts; therefore, these are the criteria that are considered when a venture capital firm in Germany decides whether to invest in a digital platform start-up.

10.2.2 Secondary Criteria

In the context of the investment decision, scalability (Q2) is also of central importance and can thus be considered a relevant investment criterion. The relevance of scalability, however, is not as pronounced as that of the previously cited criteria since only three of the four experts mentioned this criterion.

10.2.3 Tertiary Criteria

The criteria of well-known investors (Q6) and financial data (Q7) were each cited and confirmed by only two experts, so these are less strongly weighted criteria.

10.2.4 Non-criteria

Considering that only one expert cited the criterion location (Q8) in the context of the study, it is impossible to confirm that it is a relevant criterion and cannot be used as a relevant investment criterion for venture capital (VC) investors who are considering investing in digital platform startups in Germany.

It should be noted that the revenue growth criterion (H1) was not cited by anyone in this study and is therefore not able to be confirmed as a criterion for making investment decisions.

10.2.5 Conclusion

In summary, the hypotheses Q3, Q4, and Q5 have been confirmed in detail by the experts and we consider them to be venture capital (VC) investment criteria in the particular context of digital platforms, which this study is exploring. The hypothesis Q2 was confirmed by three of the four experts and can therefore be considered a VC investment criterion. Considering that only half of the experts mentioned their relevance in the decision-making process, hypotheses Q6 and Q7 can be regarded as less important investment criteria. It is not possible to confirm hypotheses Q1 and Q8.

In our empirical study, we confirm that the following investment criteria are indeed, as indicated in secondary literature, dominant factors in venture capital decision-making and funding success: (1) founders and/or management teams, (2) innovative ideas, (3) market characteristics, and (4) scalability. In the context of this study, well-known investors, financial data, sales growth, and location cannot be considered to be dominant factors in decision-making.

Based on the comparison of the empirical study findings with the derivations of the exemplary successful and unsuccessful German platform startups listed in Chap. 3, the empirical results confirm that these factors make or break success. Based on publicly available information, it was possible to conclude that digital platform start-ups that successfully attracted financing met the following criteria when it came to the successful realization of financing: innovative business idea, digitalization advances into traditional areas, competitive positioning, (international) scalability, development of the entrepreneurial and technological edge, existence of USPs, unique product and service offerings.

According to our empirical study, these criteria are consistent with what experts have stated. The development of the necessary structures and networks will also be decisive in attracting financing, since this development will enable the creation of a critical mass and thereby a perceptible size on the market. Additionally, the empirical findings confirmed the reasons for the failure of the unsuccessful digital platform start-ups discussed in Chap. 3. This failure was largely caused by the limitations of the market, the superiority of a competitor, and the limited growth potential of the company.

The research question we posed regarding the criteria a digital platform start-up must meet to obtain equity financing through VC in Germany can be considered as answered. According to analysis of the expert interviews, a digital platform start-up must have a good, high-quality management team and an innovative idea in order to obtain equity financing through venture capital in Germany. Additionally, digital platform start-ups must consider the essential characteristics of the market when developing a strategy, and they must present these characteristics to VC investors accordingly. The next section elaborates on this point.

Accordingly, given the above empirical evidence, digital platform start-ups should develop a target profile based on the above criteria in order to obtain venture capital funding. Consequently, we suggest that start-ups that meet the above criteria stand a greater chance of obtaining venture capital funding.

10.3 Implications for Venture Capital Strategy

We present the following recommendations for action in relation to digital platform start-ups, based on the results of the empirical study and the findings presented earlier. The recommendations should therefore enable a supportive orientation to be implemented in Germany as part of a strategy to achieve equity financing through venture capital (VC). As a VC investor, practical experience suggests which aspects need to be considered in developing a financing strategy for digital platform start-ups. This is in line with research on innovation, disruption and digital transformation. (Friesendorf and Uedelhoven, 2021; Friesendorf and Stern, 2020).

Please note that the information provided here should not be construed as definitive. In this way, they serve as indications of principle that can be incorporated into the practical design of a financing strategy. In the following, we have included only the confirmed criteria; location and revenue growth have been excluded.

10.3.1 Skillset and Team Structure

Based on the empirical findings of this study, the founding/management team of digital platform startups is an important determinant of the realization of equity financing by venture capitalists. It may be beneficial for digital platform start-up companies to consider the following points as practical recommendations when developing equity financing strategies. As part of the development and design of their VC fundraising strategy, digital platform start-ups have to place a great deal of emphasis on their founding and management teams as part of their VC fundraising strategy. To begin with, it is best to structure the team in such a way that each member of the team has fundamentally different skills, and ideally, there should be at least three complementary founders on the team. There is no doubt that having people with knowledge of technology, marketing, and sales is essential to the success of the company. Not only are these skills necessary to deal with technological processes, but they are also essential to bring customers to the platform once it becomes visible on the market in order to grow revenue.

10.3.2 Sales Mapping

There should be a detailed mapping of the sales area within the team, since VC investors will not invest in the company if this area has not been sufficiently developed and has not shown significant progress over a short period of time. The inadequate design of the sales areas would be one of the main reasons for rejection from the perspective of a VC investor. It is therefore essential that the sales team has a lot of experience in the sales sector.

10.3.3 Team Dynamics in Hardships

A venture capital firm should also be able to demonstrate a harmonious internal relationship to demonstrate its credibility. Therefore, this aspect should be considered when establishing the dynamics of the internal team behind the venture capital firm. Furthermore, it is crucial that the team has the drive and ambition to see the idea through to its completion, so it is also essential that the team is capable of handling stressful and difficult situations to reach the goal. Prior to the start of the project, the team should have dealt with problems and difficult phases internally before the start of the project. To be able to judge the team's ability to perform when faced with a situation that differs from normal business operations, VC investors expect some evidence of team dynamics.

10.3.4 Dynamic Capabilities

Investors in the venture capital sector place a lot of emphasis on developing a high-quality team with experience and knowledge, especially during the early phases of a company's development, such as the seed phase; however, this factor remains particularly important in the later stages of the company's development when the team will show more quality. To be able to obtain financing in later phases, it is therefore necessary for the founding team or management team to continue to gain knowledge, either through independent study or through hiring additional staff, in order to be able to apply for financing in the future. A VC investor looks for this ability in the founders and/or management team before investing in them.

10.3.5 Drive for Innovativeness

As the access to capital is not easy for start-ups who provide digital platforms, the start-up must have a fundamentally innovative business plan in order to develop a financing strategy to attract venture capitalists. It may be difficult for a platform to access capital if investors are not clear about what makes the platform stand out from its competitors in this market as a result of its innovative idea. Thus, it is essential that a good, existing, innovative idea be presented clearly in order to be considered for investment by venture capital investors, because only when VC investors believe in the idea will it be funded.

10.3.6 Elucidation of Unique Selling Proposition

As VC investors consider ideas with flaws as exclusion criteria, potential flaws should be corrected or compensated for by the company to avoid exclusion from the competition. Investors expect digital platform start-ups to highlight their unique selling propositions and explain how they are better than their competitors, as well as what problems they solve, to attract VC investors.

10.3.7 Problem-Solving Approach

For venture capital investors to be sure that a digital platform start-up's strategy is viable, the digital platform start-up must make sure that the problem that the platform is supposed to solve has been solved and that there are sufficient buyers for the solution, ensuring that the viability of a concept is always closely related to the characteristics of the market.

10.3.8 Indispensability of Online Market

According to market characteristics, it is possible to make the following recommendations for action: Digital platform start-ups should first explain to investors why they believe the offline market needs to be replaced by the online market. Additionally, they should be able to prove whether there are similar platforms in their own or adjacent markets that are capable of covering their own market or niche market in the future, as well as whether similar platforms are available in their own or adjacent markets.

10.3.9 Niche-Market Value

A start-up must also be able to demonstrate that the market that they are entering is sufficiently interesting, large, and growing in order to succeed. Additionally, investors should be informed as to where exactly the market is located and which niche it serves, if any, in order to make a more informed decision. It would be ideal for the platform to demonstrate to investors that it already has a corresponding product, either a minimum viable product or an end product, that has already shown its ability to perform in the market and has already proven its viability. When it comes to VC, digitalization should be concentrated on areas that are not highly competitive from a VC point of view.

10.3.10 Expected Customer Growth, Retention, and Churn Rate

In the context of financial data, it would not be possible to make any recommendations for taking any action in the short term. Since the data used as the basis for business plans in the early stages of VC are largely meaningless, this is the case, as the data used as the basis for business plans are relatively meaningless. The business plan, however, should be written in such a way as to give investors a sense of how the founders think and how they plan to scale their business. The key performance indicators should be included in financial data as a matter of principle. It is essential for startups to explain where exactly customer growth occurs, why the churn rate is so high, how long customers stay on the platform, and how often they buy and sell on the platform. If VC investors have more precise information about the units of economics and the customer retention rate of the digital platform start-up, they will be more able to evaluate the effectiveness of the business model for the digital platform start-up.

10.3.11 Clarification of Scalability Potential

There is no doubt that the concept of scalability can be summarized in the following way: Once a start-up has a large number of users on its platform, it will be able to scale very quickly as well as gain investors' interest very quickly, since high valuations of a company will also be associated with high scalability. Scalability recommendations are influenced by the perception of growth opportunities by VC investors. A platform's rapid scaling is a prerequisite for reducing the chances of competitors entering the market, particularly at the beginning. Rapid scaling, on the other hand, allows VC investors to determine whether the platform will be able to scale within a short period of time. As a result, platforms should demonstrate to VC investors how they can scale and where growth opportunities exist.

10.3.12 Track Record of Venture Capital Investor

A start-up with a well-known track record should also look for financing from venture capitalists with a well-established track record, since investing in a start-up with a well-known investor offers benefits both from a reputational perspective and from a strategic perspective to the investor.

10.3.13 Team-Building and Long-Term Skill-Planning

If a digital platform start-up is looking for financing at an early stage and has developed criteria that are decisive from a VC perspective, the following recommendations are a good place to start. Starting a digital platform company is a great opportunity for its team to be equipped with many different skills from the beginning, specifically sales talent and sales force.

Furthermore, the uniqueness of the digital platform must also be clearly communicated to VC investors in order to convince them that this idea and platform are superior to those of their competitors. The market characteristics will also have to be described, including how the competitors are doing, and why the company needs to move away from the offline market in order to succeed. Finally, and perhaps most importantly, it is important to clearly state where scaling potential lies and what further growth opportunities exist in the future.

Ultimately, no matter how far one goes into detail, it is thc tcam that matters most, as INT 2 pointed out: "Yes, exactly." I mean, you can go into as much detail as you like, of course, about everything we pay attention to. But I think the team is the most important thing." (cf. INT 2, 00:27:47, lines 344–346)

10.4 Implications for Research

At the beginning of 2022, there were 25 unicorns in Germany according to the German government's latest publication on the start-up ecosystem known as the "Start-up-Strategie der Bundesregierung," which together accounted for a market value of at least $1 billion. Both the German government and the European Commission have set a goal of doubling the number of "unicorns" in Europe by 2030. There has been a general lack of attention given to start-ups by politicians and policymakers until recently, but this is changing rapidly. This is because there is a broader perception that startups are the inventors of new ideas, the innovators of market disruption, and the pioneers of innovative thinking, which is why there is a bias towards them. We can expect a dramatic change in the German start-up ecosystem in the coming months, because of the urgent need to address product and factor market deficits both in Germany and across Europe.

The German federal government announced in July 2022 a comprehensive start-up strategy aimed at improving the conditions for start-ups in the country. This strategy consists of ten areas of action and has the objective of improving the start-up financing options, facilitating spin-offs from science, improving the framework conditions for public welfare-oriented start-ups, and mobilizing public contracting competencies. There has also been a clear commitment by both the national and state governments of Germany to encourage start-up initiatives, particularly in universities, partnering with companies to create jobs as well as strengthen the competitiveness of the economy through the development of knowledge-based products and services. As a result, the rise of startups has gained recognition as a significant source of innovation in response to new challenges such as climate neutrality and the transition to renewable energy sources.

In view of these developments, we believe that our study will be able to contribute and facilitate not just the decision-making of entrepreneurs and venture capitalists, but also that of policymakers. The purpose of our research is to provide insight into equity financing options and alternative financing methods for both economic research and entrepreneurship practice in the future. It might be of interest to conduct future research that focuses on adding to our list of funding criteria, particularly for startups with digital platforms that are able to take advantage of technological advancements while enabling stakeholder efficiency while taking advantage of technological advancements.

By separating literature-guided approaches from inductive research with many representatives in order to obtain a deeper understanding of investment selection and investment criteria on the basis of methodologies, we can gain a more detailed understanding of investment selection and investment criteria. In addition to providing support for the development of more comprehensive financing strategies for start-ups in the digital platform industry, and for start-ups in general, these results could also provide support for the development of more comprehensive financing strategies for start-ups in general in Germany. As the government, it would be especially helpful if such research could contribute to the development of a new ecosystem and industry, as well as serving the welfare interests of the state by providing employment opportunities.

The results of this study are also indicative of the need for further research to determine whether the same investment criteria are applied in deciding whether to invest in a start-up in a different part of the world, outside of Germany, and thereby to gain knowledge of regional venture capital investors' investment criteria. We believe that by doing so, we will be able to enhance the competitiveness of the European market and we will be able to facilitate the creation of a socioeconomic transformation that can be replicated in different regions of the world.

Also, future research approaches may be able to assist start-ups not only in developing digital platforms but also in developing financing strategies that will help start-ups develop their own digital platforms. In the best-case scenario, it will result in economic, technological, and innovative progress, as well as knowledge of investment criteria used by venture capitalists who provide equity capital, which will, in turn, lead to economic, technological, and innovative advancement. There is no doubt that the start-up industry in Europe will continue to grow, and it will be a thriving area of knowledge, skill, and success for many years to come.

10.5 Implications for General Practice

We provide herewith some practical tips based on the latest developments pushed forth by the German Federal Government that aims to set up a flourishing start-up ecosystem with private equity and venture capital avenues. In the future, there will be private and public funding available for setting up start-ups based on digital and AI technologies. Access to this could be easier if some of the following points are integrated into the financing strategy of the start-up.

In order to strengthen female founders and diversity among start-up companies, the German government is developing a comprehensive instrument as part of the Future Fund, namely Zukunftsfond. This instrument is targeted at management teams newly exposed to venture capital (VC). They are supported in raising funds for their start-up through an investment from Zukunftsfonds. Specifically, women, migrants, and other groups that have been underrepresented in the venture capital market will have better access to it. The funding of female and diverse venture capital funds will have a multiplier effect and improve access to venture capital for female founders and diverse teams.

As part of the EXIST funding program—Start-ups from Science—the German government intends to provide more support for female founders and establish a new funding line titled "EXIST Women." Mixed teams will be preferred since diversified start-up teams are more likely to succeed in the long run. There will be a higher network allowance for universities to support and coach diverse teams. If a female mentor is selected by the founding team, an additional increase is provided. This program is designed to encourage female professors to become mentors and to increase their visibility as role models.

The EXIST start-up teams will in the future receive an extension of their funding if they have a child born to a member of the team. A new dedicated funding line for women, "EXIST Women," will also be established by the federal government to facilitate the transition of women founders to self-employment and sustainably increase the participation of women in all team constellations.

The German government intends to significantly increase the number of women serving on the investment committees of state funds and investment companies. By appointing gender-balanced members to the High-Tech Gründerfonds investment committee, the Federal Ministry of Economics and Climate Protection aims to achieve its gender parity goal.

The German government will strengthen the "FRAUEN unternehmen" (Women in Business) initiative by appointing more female role models in the STEM fields. It is hoped that this initiative will demonstrate to schoolgirls, students, and young women in particular that professional independence is also a viable option for women.

The federal government will establish a forum for migrants to network with other start-ups, established companies, and scientific institutions. It is hoped that this will serve as the beginning of a long-term process for strengthening the integration of international founders into the start-up ecosystem. In this way, the German government hopes to encourage greater cooperation between migrant startups. Migrant startups face many challenges, including bureaucratic obstacles, language barriers, and a lack of networks.

Germany plans to introduce a "Leuchtturmwettbewerb Entrepreneurship-Zentren" (entrepreneurial competition) to supplement its "EXIST Potentials" funding program. In order to establish cross-university ecosystems with international appeal and strong integration into regional and national value chains, five to ten excellence-oriented projects with long duration are planned for funding.

The German government will provide more assistance and support in the transfer of intellectual property (IP) in the future and will promote standard solutions (e.g., "IP for virtual shares") as well as setting up an arbitration board (initially as a pilot project) with a deal database that will facilitate transparency and reduce disputes in the future. The aim of this initiative is to link the promotion of science start-ups with the wide application of these standard IP transfer solutions, as well as continue the process of developing best-practice solutions for IP transfer that has already been initiated by science institutions, start-ups, transfer organizations, and other interested parties.

It is intended that the Federal Government will intensify its dialogue with the Länder, i.e. the state governments on the subject of founding structures at universities and other research institutions that are not universities. The focus will be on improving support for those who wish to start their own businesses and developing a more creative, risk-taking culture within the institutions. At a minimum, pro rata funding should be provided to students and researchers for awareness raising and entrepreneurship training.

The German government will work with the states to examine how to achieve permanence and sustainable funding for the necessary measures and structures that have already been created through joint initiatives such as the federal-state program "Innovative Hochschule" to strengthen transfer, known as the "3rd mission." (Deutscher Bundestag, 2022)

Furthermore, the Federal Government will work with the Länder in order to determine how existing obstacles to spin-offs can be systematically identified and addressed, and how incentive structures can be improved in order to encourage more spin-offs to occur. A particular focus of the German government will be to facilitate the exchange of best practices regarding the process of supporting university start-ups.

With the EXIST workshops, the Federal Government intends to enhance the exchange between universities and non-university research institutions and experts focusing on practice-oriented exchange as well as supplement the workshops with topic-related individual formats, such as those relating to state aid law or alumni involvement.

In cooperation with stakeholders, the German government is seeking to look at ways to make it easier for different disciplines to better network at an early stage, such as creating interdisciplinary start-up teams by bringing together students in STEM courses with business economists. It is expected that the federal government will simplify the process for awarding public tenders and procuring goods for educational institutions as well. This will remove obstacles for startups in Government and Education Technology (INT 2, 2021).

Considering the above developments, start-up stakeholders should take some or all of the above requirements into consideration and build their network of research, universities, state agencies, incumbents, and the media in order to increase their eligibility and their chances of receiving funding for their companies by integrating some or all of the above requirements. As a result of our analysis, we are confident that the German start-up ecosystem as well as the private equity and VC markets will be able to demonstrate strong growth trends for years to come. Our best wishes are extended out to all stakeholders for the success of their endeavors.

References

Deutscher Bundestag. (2022). *Start-up-Strategie der Bundesregierung*. https://dserver.bundestag.de/btd/20/030/2003063.pdf

Friesendorf, C., & Stern, J. (2020). Mangelnde Digitalisierung in der Finanzbranche. In *Digitalisierung des Auslandszahlungsverkehrs. essentials*. Springer. https://doi.org/10.1007/978-3-658-32738-5_1

Friesendorf, C., & Uedelhoven, L. (2021). Digital transformation of global mobility markets. In *Mobility in Germany. Springer briefs in business*. Springer. https://doi.org/10.1007/978-3-030-71849-7_1

INT 2. (2021, August 27). *Transcript of the expert interview*.

MIX
Papier aus verantwortungsvollen Quellen
Paper from responsible sources
FSC® C105338

If you have any concerns about our products,
you can contact us on
ProductSafety@springernature.com

In case Publisher is established outside the EU,
the EU authorized representative is:
Springer Nature Customer Service Center GmbH
Europaplatz 3, 69115 Heidelberg, Germany

Printed by Libri Plureos GmbH
in Hamburg, Germany